MW00834785

▶ **Reclaiming Poch@ Pop**

DOI: 10.1057/9781137498076.0001

Latino Pop Culture

Series Editor: **Frederick Luis Aldama**

Books in the series give serious critical attention to all facets of Latino popular culture. Books focus on topics generally that pertain to the making and consuming of Latino pop culture, including music, performance and body art, TV shows, film, comic books, web media, pop art, low-riders, sartorial wear, video games, sports, and cuisine, among many other areas.

Titles include:

Cruz Medina
RECLAIMING POCH@ POP
Examining the Rhetoric of Cultural Deficiency

Frederick Luis Aldama and Christopher González
LATINOS IN THE END ZONE
Conversations on the Brown Color Line in the NFL

DOI: 10.1057/9781137498076.0001

palgrave▸pivot

Reclaiming Poch@ Pop: Examining the Rhetoric of Cultural Deficiency

Cruz Medina
Santa Clara University, USA

palgrave
macmillan

DOI: 10.1057/9781137498076.0001

RECLAIMING POCH@ POP
Copyright © Cruz Medina, 2015.

Foreword © Arturo Aldama, 2015.
Cartoons courtesy Lalo Alcaraz & Universal Uclick syndicate Copyright 2014

Permission for images from *Codex Espangliensis: From Columbus to the Border Patrol* provided by Felicia Rice at Moving Parts Press.

All rights reserved.

First published in 2015 by
PALGRAVE MACMILLAN®
in the United States—a division of St. Martin's Press LLC,
175 Fifth Avenue, New York, NY 10010.

Where this book is distributed in the UK, Europe and the rest of the world, this is by Palgrave Macmillan, a division of Macmillan Publishers Limited, registered in England, company number 785998, of Houndmills, Basingstoke, Hampshire RG21 6XS.

Palgrave Macmillan is the global academic imprint of the above companies and has companies and representatives throughout the world.

Palgrave® and Macmillan® are registered trademarks in the United States, the United Kingdom, Europe and other countries.

ISBN: 978–1–137–49813–7 EPUB
ISBN: 978–1–137–49807–6 PDF
ISBN: 978–1–137–50157–8 Hardback

Library of Congress Cataloging-in-Publication Data is available from the Library of Congress.

A catalogue record of the book is available from the British Library.

First edition: 2015

www.palgrave.com/pivot

DOI: 10.1057/9781137498076

For Kathryn, William Julian, and Jackson.
And to Julian and Debra for their sacrifices.

DOI: 10.1057/9781137498076.0001

Contents

DOI: 10.1057/9781137498076.0001

List of Figures

Foreword

Arturo J. Aldama

To frame my discussion of *Poch@ Pop*, I start with drawing attention to two points that are argued throughout *The Darker Side of the Renaissance: Literacy, Territoriality, and Colonization* (University of Michigan, 2003) by Walter Mignolo. First, he contends that the Spanish/European conquest of Mexico and the Americas was based and practiced on absolute denial of the "coevalness" of Indigenous civilizations with European cultures and empires; and he argues that the contemporary "postcolonial" condition that frames borderlands studies is characterized by a sustained attempt to "deny" the "denial of the coevalness" of civilizations. Second, his book challenges scholars and activist intellectuals to consider the complex enunciative, epistemic, and discursive practices in borderlands loci that are grounded in layered indigenous epistemologies and cultural practices. It is in the epistemic space to deny the denial of coevalness that Cruz Medina practices a nuanced, multilayered, and multi-genre intervention in US-México popular cultural studies. Through a series of decolonial ruptures and articulations, *Poch@ Pop* skillfully re-locates a subject position/rhetorical position/and epistemic space of the Pocha and Pocho or Poch@ (to queer and problematize binary gender endings of masculine and feminine in Spanish). Dr. Medina metaphorically lifts the bucket of the term Pocho and its history of negative connotations (not Mexican enough, not authentic, impure, fractured, traitor, diglossic, etc.) and its complex origins in Mesoamerican

DOI: 10.1057/9781137498076.0003

societies (pochteca) and flips it over and embraces the layered elegance of contemporary Poch@ cultural expressions. *Poch@ Pop* embraces a Poch@ subject, looks at Pocho cultural productions and offers a compelling methodology of how to read Poch@ aesthetics, and destroys or at least attempts to destroy the rhetoric of deficiency associated with the term Poch@.

Medina takes on a ludic—sometimes funny—and always nuanced look at the Poch@ cultural and narrative practices and rhetorical performances in a range of genres and with a range of cutting-edge borderlands cultural producers. His writing is elegant, clear, and will speak to scholars, consumers, and producers of popular culture, film, graphic novels, music, and performance art. Framed against the current political backdrop of xenophobia and nativist intolerance of borders, and border crossings by mestizo@ subjects, *Poch@ Pop* offers the readers a six-chapter look at how artists resist "rhetorics of cultural deficiency" and looks at such poch@ popsters as Ritchie Valens, Selena Quintanilla-Pérez, Tejano filmmaker Roberto Rodriguez, cartoonist Lalo Alcaraz, performance artist Guillermo Gómez-Peña, actor and director Edward James Olmos, Luis Valdez, icon of Chicano theatre and film, Al Madrigal commentator on the *Daily Show*, actor and art promoter, Cheech Marin, and the well regarded music group, Ozomatli.

Inspired by the decolonial possibilities articulated by Gloria Anzaldua's classic, *Borderlands/La Frontera*, *Poch@ Pop* is part of a new and cutting-edge wave and way to read borderlands cultural productions. *Poch@ Pop* should be taught, used, and enjoyed in large classes, graduate seminars, and faculty reading groups and in community centers and spaces. It will make a fine *vecino* (neighbor) in the barrio of your bookshelf next to such works as *Tex(t)-Mex: Seductive Hallucinations of the "Mexican" in America* (Univ. of Texas Press, 2007) by William Anthony Nericcio, *Wild Tongues: Transnational Mexican Popular Culture* by Rita E. Urquijo-Ruiz (Univ. of Texas Press, 2012), *Performing the US Latina and Latino Borderlands*, Eds. Arturo J. Aldama, Chela Sandoval, and Peter J. Garcia (Indiana Univ. Press, 2012) and the very recently released *Creating Aztlán: Chicano Art, Indigenous Sovereignty, and Lowriding across Turtle Island* by Dylan A.T. Miner (Univ. of Arizona Press, 2014) among many other engaging and tour de force books.

I end my enthusiastic foreword by citing directly from *Poch@ Pop*. I chose this passage because it is a particularly poetic and uplifting

DOI: 10.1057/9781137498076.0003

celebration of Poch@s and Poch@ pop rhetoric in the Afterword inspired by the author's *encuentro* with the iconic Cheech Marin:

> I hope this book reaffirms the strength of poch@ pop rhetoric as well as reminds audiences that the struggles of dehumanizing rhetoric is ongoing. Poch@ pop passes out political tacos at the sit-ins and demonstrations where poch@ tunes lift the heavy hearts and fists, pounding out the beat in time to the brush strokes of murals depicting the imminent demise of global DC and Disney empires … I say *si poch@s pueden.*

The only thing I will add is that *soy poch@ y que*!!!

DOI: 10.1057/9781137498076.0003

Acknowledgments

I would first like to thank the series editor Frederick Luis Aldama for his interest and enthusiasm in the project. Thanks to Santa Clara University's Inclusive Excellence Postdoctoral Fellowship for the time and space to work. Thanks to Texas State University-San Marcos Pre-doctoral Fellowship which facilitated my archival research at the Benson Latin American Collection at University of Texas at Austin.

I must acknowledge my family and everyone who has helped me and provided me with intellectual insights and emotional support. This work exists because of the sacrifices by many who came before me. I thank my paternal grandparents, Julian and Dorothy "Dot" Medina, for putting my father Julian through two years of seminary and encouraging him to continue with his Master's degree in English when he wanted to quit. I thank my father, Julian, and keep his memory close as the first of his family to go to college and then teach English at the community college level for more than 20 years. I remember my mother's parents and thank them for raising my mother to be the first of her family to go to college; and I thank my mother, Debra, whose example as a strong woman, teacher, and lover of culture and life affects me more than I recognize and am sometimes willing to admit. Thanks to Z for being my big brother who's always led the way. Thank you to my spouse and "teammate," Kathryn, who has been with me through the twists and turns of grad school, reminding me to enjoy life and celebrate accomplishments.

I thank my colleagues and former professors at the University of Arizona who mentored a creative writer

DOI: 10.1057/9781137498076.0004

turned rhet/comp-er. Thank you, Anne-Marie Hall, for guiding me early on in my coursework. *Gracias*, Adela C. Licona for our one-on-one talks—I hope you know how much I appreciate your guidance, mentorship, and friendship. Thank you, Damián Baca, for serving as my dissertation chair and mentor, and for providing a prolific writing model.

I'd like to thank everyone who's read versions of this project. *Gracias*, Cristina Ramirez for your insights on clear, punchy writing. *Gracias*, Juan Gallegos for your interest in the future of poch@ studies. *Gracias*, William A. Nericcio—I will always remain a *Tex[t]-Mex* blog fanboy. *Gracias a mi hermana academica*, Aja Martinez, for all the early career advice and for your thoughts on this project. *Gracias* to my Santa Clara *compañero* and mentor, Juan Velasco, whose writing always inspires me to raise analysis to the level of poetry. For all the writing feedback: Kenneth Walker and Erica Cirillo McCarthy.

Thank you, Ed White, your storytelling continues to impact how I narrate my life. Thank you, Erec Toso—I aspire to teach as you taught me. Thank you, Randy and Constance at the Little Chapel—yours is the best water and positive energy in my Tucson. Much love to the New Start Summer Bridge Program.

Thanks to my Latina/o Caucus *gente*! *Gracias* Victor Villanueva for your writing, leadership, and for your model as scholar-teacher. Abrazos to Aja Martinez—my academic big-sister; Sonia Arellano, Ana Ribero, and José Cortez—my academic sisters and brother—y'all surprise and amaze me with your work and futures. Natalie Martinez, *mi prima melancholia*. *Gracias* Octavio Pimentel, you're the Jay-Z to my Kanye, bringing me out to San Marcos and letting me write, while schooling me with your mentoring. Jaime Armin Mejía—*muchas gracias* for your generous feedback and support—it has meant and continues to mean so much. *Gracias* Cristina Kirklighter, Renee Moreno, Cecilia Rodriguez Milanes, and Isabel Baca—I appreciate your strong and caring leadership in addition to your wonderful writing. Enrique Reynoso, I never tire of your wit and depths of obscure pop culture knowledge.

Thank you to my colleagues at Santa Clara University—special thanks to Simone Billings, John Hawley, and Eileen Elrod for believing in me. Thanks to Julia Voss and Tricia Serviss, my fellow rhet/comp cohort; my mentors: Diane Dreher, Pedro Hernández-Ramos, and Juan Velasco. And *muchos abrazos* and thanks to everyone in the LEAD scholars program.

DOI: 10.1057/9781137498076.0004

1

A Poch@ Pop Preface:
Si se puede

Abstract: *Chapter 1 introduces poch@ as the growing Latin@ audience in the U.S. and those pop culture artists who reflect their experiences. Autobiographical material about the author illuminates intersections among popular culture, humor, and political and social realities. The trope of pocho, pocha, or poch@ reemerges as a self-identifier for Latin@ pop culture producers who respond and resist rhetoric framing Latin@s as deficient.*

Medina, Cruz. *Reclaiming Poch@ Pop: Examining the Rhetoric of Cultural Deficiency.* New York: Palgrave Macmillan, 2015. DOI: 10.1057/9781137498076.0005.

When I first saw Dolores Huerta give the keynote address at a conference on decolonization at the University of Arizona, I took a "selfie" with her after she spoke. Huerta's keynote followed her highly criticized talk at Tucson Magnet High School, where she told students that "Republicans don't care about Latinos." At that moment of *kairos*, Huerta's critique of Arizona's ultraconservative legislators was apropos in the light of Senate Bill 1070, which legalized the racial-profiling of Latinas/os suspected of being "illegal." While the policy of SB 1070 called the citizenship of all Latinas/os into question through the heightened policing of Latinas/os bodies, Huerta's criticism would be later attacked in the political theater to support outlawing Mexican American Studies (MAS) at Tucson Magnet High School via House Bill (HB) 2281. The rhetoric of HB 2281 misrepresented the MAS program as promoting "governmental overthrow" and "resentment of different races," even though the logic of higher state test scores and graduation rates demonstrated the efficacy of the culturally relevant curriculum and social justice pedagogy[1].

I begin with the persuasiveness of Huerta's oratory, which has moved generations of audiences to act since the formation of the United Farm Workers' union with Cesar Chavez, because Huerta's speech that day has personal reverberations in popular culture. In her address, Huerta

FIGURE 1.1   *Dolores Huerta with Medina*

DOI: 10.1057/9781137498076.0005

explained that the now-iconic phrase "*Sí se puede*" emerged during her activist work of going door-to-door to register voters. When many of the people with whom she spoke said "*no puedo* (no, I can't)," she responded "*Sí, se puede* (yes you can)." In my own home, I need go no further than my two year-old son's *Go, Diego, Go!* (2007) compact disc with a song entitled "Si Se Puede" to see a connection with Huerta's phrase and pop culture. Despite the appropriation of the slogan in the realm of pop culture, *si se puede* continues to serve as a rhetorical rallying cry to challenge political issues affecting Latinas/os.

In reality, I admit that after I heard Huerta's story, I joked with a Chicana colleague that I had always thought that the phrase had come from the same source from where all great things Chicana/o originated: Edward James Olmos. For readers of this book, that joke should ring true to some extent because Olmos has been the figure who has transgressed pop culture genres including iconic roles in *Zoot Suit* (1981), *Blade Runner* (1982), *Miami Vice* (1984–1990), *Stand and Deliver* (1988), *American Me* (1992), *My Family* (1995), *Selena* (1997), *American Family* (2002), and the *Battlestar Galactica* TV series (2004–2009), to name a few. Because pop culture plays an intrinsic role in how culture is discussed in the U.S., mainstream pop culture is often the common referent for Latina/o and non-Latina/o audiences, as it often is for non-Latina/o audiences. For Latina/o pop culture consumers in the U.S., Edward James Olmos has represented the street-wise pachuco watching their backs, the strong role model as teacher, head of family, and captain on intergalactic voyages traversing the collective pop cultural memory. Olmos' presence challenges the racist punchline for the joke about "why there were no Latinas/os on *Star Trek*," by proving that Latinas/os want to work, and *do* in fact work in the future. More importantly, many of the television programs and films that Olmos has starred in have marked temporal signposts for many Latina/o audiences in the U.S.

I still recall when I was eight years old and I saw *Stand and Deliver* (1988) in theaters twice. For my family, the film inspired a sense of pride. Both of my parents were educators: my mother taught English as a Second Language (ESL) at my elementary school and my father taught English at a Hispanic-Serving community college. Therefore, Olmos' portrayal of real-life educator Jaime Escalante, the East Los Angeles math teacher, who excelled in the preparation of Latina/o students for the advanced placement calculus exam, shone a positive light on the ignored efforts of Latina/o teachers and students. For me, it represented the success in

DOI: 10.1057/9781137498076.0005

school that was mirrored back at me by students who looked like me and the kids on my schoolyard. Some critics have reductively categorized *Stand and Deliver* as a so-called "social problems" film that promotes the rhetoric that social and political issues only require limited change.[2] Still, my family no doubt returned for a second viewing in theaters because my parents valued the broader-reaching implications from the radically local microcosm of a single classroom. And while I recognize the potential dangerous interpretation of the film as promoting the bootstrap rhetoric that Victor Villanueva[3] exposes as counterproductive for communities of color, I proceed with this discussion because the rhetoric of pop culture inspires, as it entertains, and disrupts oppressive narratives that dominate political and material discourse communities. Jokes aside, pop culture like *Stand and Deliver* interrupts dominant political and social rhetoric by reaffirming to Latinas/os that they can achieve with the important message of: *si se puede*.

Los nombres de nomenclature

Recently, more attention has been paid to Latinas/os for political and economic purposes. In the 2012 presidential election, the "Latino vote" served as something of a topos, or rhetorical commonplace, that political analysts integrated into their talking points. Similarly, the projected doubling of the population of people with Latin American heritage in the U.S. by 2050 has functioned as a call to action by educators working to develop culturally responsive curriculum and pedagogy to the needs of this growing population.[4] Discussions of political agency and education, however, continue to paint Latin@s with a broad brush that reinforces the assumption of a false monolith—ignoring the diversity and broad spectrum of identities and experiences. A part of this monolith assumption was a resurgence of the "sleeping giant" voting metaphor when Mitt Romney courted the "Latino vote" too late in the 2012 election, a metaphor that Rudolpho Acuña rejects as "anesthetizing."[5] The sleeping giant remains a rhetorical trope in the context of politics because it recognizes "minorities" without necessarily enacting policy that shifts power in acknowledgment of majority-status population demographics.

At this point, it might be helpful to acknowledge the trope of pocha/o from which I extrapolate and identify the rhetorical power of primarily-English-speaking Latina/o pop culture producers in the U.S.

DOI: 10.1057/9781137498076.0005

Until now, there have been canonical representations of pocha/o as a trope that signifies "cultural traitor."[6] The cultural traitor connotation of pocha/o does little to demonstrate how the trope of poch@ has come to symbolize resistance through the efforts of the pop culture producers who self-identify with it—from here I will write simply "@" instead of "a/o" to demonstrate inclusivity, rather than the a/o construction that reinforces an either/or colonial binary. In most cases, I also break from the use of "o\a" and "a\o" when writing Latino\a, Latina\o, Chicana\o and Chicano\a, which has been found by Chican@ scholars to maintain a rigid binary for gender and sexuality,[7] while the "@" performs a visual and queered representation of inclusivity. With regard to self-identification, I use the "@" sign as a part of the transgressive and decolonial stance that poch@ embodies. At the same time, the spiral image conjures up images of the snake eating itself, the very same image Anzaldúa uses in conversation with Andrea Lunsford to describe the counter-knowledge of *conocimiento*.[8] This image aptly symbolizes how her work concerning colonial borders of identity, mestiza consciousness, and the incorporation of Pre-Columbian tropes informs what I identify as poch@ pop.

To discuss poch@ requires a necessary explanation of how the trope fits into the greater spectrum of pan-ethnic nomenclatures. Recent Pew research found that the majority of people of Latin American heritage first identify their ethnicity with their country of origin, and then by pan-ethnic nomenclature such as Hispanic or Latin@.[9] The rhetorical erasure of difference is often dismissed by oversimplified critiques of "political correctness," so I submit poch@ as a nomenclature like Chican@ that seeks to right the wrongs played out in politics. I have admittedly heard dismissals from my more conservative-leaning Mexican American family members who say things like, "Latino, Chicano, Hispanic? What's the difference? I don't know what to call them—they're changing what to call themselves all the time." Not only is the use of "them" as opposed to "us" problematic, but the rhetorical question also highlights an underlying fallacy revealed in the assumed, commonly-held belief of the argument. The assertion arrived at by this enthymeme sounds correct, though the logic is spurious. It is, of course, fallacious because the construction of enthymemes as incomplete syllogisms often includes false claims in the omitted universal truth or commonplace. In this case, there are political implications with all pan-ethnic nomenclatures. Following this logic, I posit that poch@ transgresses colonial and political borders that

DOI: 10.1057/9781137498076.0005

have been placed around Hispanic and Latin@, and to a lesser degree Chican@ and mestiz@.

The identifier "Hispanic" exemplifies the adage relevant to self-identification that if a group does not come up with a name for themselves, they will have one assigned to them. Even though Hispanic has roots in Nixon-era governmental racial categories, recent Pew research finds that Hispanic remains the most used pan-ethnic identifier: "half (50%) of Hispanics say they have no preference between the two…'Hispanic' is preferred to 'Latino' by two-to-one (33% versus 15% of all respondents)."[10] In this book, I identify how U.S.-born, English-dominant pop culture producers with Latin American heritage (predominantly Mexican heritage) reclaim poch@ by self-identifying with a once pejorative trope to subvert rhetoric portraying "Hispanics" or "Latinos" in the U.S. as deficient. I do so in the rhetorical tradition of Henry Louis Gates who reclaims the "slave" trope of the signifyin' monkey as a literary and political trope,[11] responding to what Kenneth Burke referred to as the "master" tropes.[12] I posit that poch@ pop producers present a more critical standpoint than what is represented in mainstream political discourse, policy, and pop culture.

Because the ethos of poch@ pop is one of inclusivity, I sometimes use Latin@ in cases where Chican@ also fits to include Latin@s who might not self-identify as Chican@ into the conversation. I use Latin@ to refer to those persons of Mexican heritage who do not identify as Chican@ because I speak through numerous points of access to the cultural memory and histories that have been erased and covered over through the process of colonization. I believe that many poch@ pop artists have come into a Chican@ consciousness that recognizes and seeks to effect change in a world with social inequality, though it is a process. It would be against the ethos of reclaiming poch@ from the colonial imaginary to reject any Latin@ or Hispanic who does not self-identify as Chican@, which is a part of the ambiguity that empowers poch@ with rhetorical power to navigate identity in different contexts with different audiences. I do not come to this decision about pan-ethnic identity easily. Having taught, researched, and written in the geographic and political space of Arizona, I am very much aware of how I am marked and implicated by legislative discourse that continues to categorize brown bodies as "undocumented," "alien," or "illegal."

Because of the policy that normalizes dehumanizing labels such as "illegal," it is necessary to focus on those cultural productions that disrupt these neocolonial narratives in public sites such as politics and

DOI: 10.1057/9781137498076.0005

media. This project on poch@ pop came about because of the resistant, irreverent, and controversial voices producing media and art who have branded themselves with poch@. Challenging the translation of "cultural traitor"[13], political cartoonist Lalo Alcaraz has embraced the term as co-editor of the *Pocho.com*'s website, host of the *Pocho Hour of Power* Radio Show, and collaborator with Pocho Productions and National Pochismo Institute. Alcaraz's social satire addresses issues affecting Latin@s such as immigration, exploitation, racism, bilingualism, and education while simultaneously complicating representations of *latinidad*[14,15]. Never shying from controversy, performance artist Guillermo Gómez-Peña has similarly reclaimed poch@ by naming his theater group La Pocha Nostra as a challenge to what he describes as out-of-date colonial categories. While producers of popular culture like Alcaraz and Gómez-Peña consciously contest mainstream representations and rhetoric that frame Latin@s as culturally deficient, this emerging poch@ tradition influences critical consumption and inspires the next generation of pop culture producers.

Rhetorical strategies of language, humor, and satire

Reclaiming Poch@ Pop examines how the once pejorative poch@ has come to serve as a symbol for resistance against enduring rhetoric of cultural deficiency[16] and colonial narratives[17] for this generation of pop culture consumers. Tracing the historical trajectory of the poch@ in pop culture, I begin with iconic films of the 1980s and 1990s—which I contextually refer to as proto-poch@ pop—to demonstrate how representations of English-speaking Latin@s broke from cliché cinematic misrepresentations. In *La Bamba* (1986), when Lou Diamond Phillips as Ritchie Valens says in his best poch@-Spanish "No *hablo* Español" to his Anglo manager, or Edward James Olmos explains to Jennifer Lopez's title character in *Selena* (1996) that she needs to be "more Mexican than the Mexicans and more American than the Americans,"[18] these films complicate assumptions about the monolithic Latin@ experience with the Spanish language and Latin@ culture. These proto-poch@ pop cinematic depictions during the late eighties and nineties demonstrate mainstream acceptance of English-speaking Latin@ performers, despite the fact that the subjects of the biographical films embrace their cultural heritage.

Still, Phillips' portrayal of Valens declaring that he does not speak Spanish touches on one of the most salient factors related to the trope

DOI: 10.1057/9781137498076.0005

of poch@: the inability to speak Spanish. Appeals to poch@ audiences reveal ideological considerations of class coded by the Spanish language; América Rodriguez explains that "the Spanish language is proxy for the 'mass' of lower socioeconomic class Hispanic audience; English language usage by Hispanics is the sign of a higher class of Hispanic audience."[19] Even though poch@s have been identified as the target market, within the fastest growing "minority" population, companies have difficulties appealing directly to this audience because of a lack of intercultural awareness. These transnational corporations may desire revenue from poch@s, although it is extremely unlikely that this will result in an enduring systemic shift in economic power. Neocolonialism persists due to unequal power relationships undergirded by rhetoric manifested into legal policy. Poch@ artists negotiate these complex messages by formulating rhetorical pop culture productions that identifies with an audience, which hegemonic systems of power prefer to subjugate rather than appeal to.

Reclaiming Poch@ Pop also examines the rhetorical strategy of humor and satire incorporated into the pop culture representations responding to rhetoric constructing Latin@s in the media and in policy as lacking knowledge, culture, history, and perhaps even the very right to be in the U.S. In the Greco-Roman rhetorical tradition, Plato touches on how humor as a genre allows the producers to remain at the margins: "We shall enjoin that such representations be left to slaves or hired aliens, and that they receive no serious consideration whatsoever. No free person, whether woman or man, shall be found taking lessons in them."[20] It comes as no surprise that Plato represents the tradition of hegemonic knowledge which informs colonial systems of power. Those in the position of power need not rely on humor when deliberative rhetoric allows them to marginalize and discredit brown bodies as "alien" and illegal.

In *Chicano Satire: A Study in Literary Culture*, Guillermo Hernández specifically speaks of poch@ while arguing that comedy and satire serve as modes for recommending Chican@ community standards through the synthesis of Mexican and Anglo cultural expectations. According to Hernández, poch@ has historically maintained a rhetorical fluidity:

> the comic or satirical usage of the term pocho may reflect the relationship between the speaker and the individual thus labeled...an intimate or familiar level [pochita]. Yet pocho may convey a derogatory meaning when employed toward a rival or an enemy.[21]

DOI: 10.1057/9781137498076.0005

The historical meaning of poch@, as a comic or satirical figure, provides a contextualized rationale for the continued rhetorical elements of humor and satire to be employed by current artists who transcend previous static definitions. Furthermore, the embodied rhetoric of the trope further underscores why poch@ pop producers challenge dominant norms and deficiency narratives such as those written into law with subversive humor and satire or re-purposed mainstream cultural productions.

Poch@ rhetoric and English studies

I begin this preface by employing autobiographical storytelling as in the Latin@ traditions of *cuentos*, *consejos*, and *testimonio* in much the same way that rhetorical scholar Victor Villanueva employs narrative while making the personal into the "public and the public personalized."[22] In addition to drawing on relevant Latin@ rhetorical traditions, I begin and return at moments to personal narrative, as with the photo of Dolores Huerta and myself, drawing on a framework of cultural materialism. I employ cultural materialism by addressing cultural artifacts with autobiographical narratives that contest, complicate, and, at times, support existing cultural narratives.[23] Following Wendy Hesford's example of writing my life into existing narratives, I investigate "how one attempts to position oneself, or is positioned, among competing discourses and that relocates autobiography in the rhetorical and historical moments of it production and reception."[24] Examining pop culture with a cultural materialist framework underscores how cultural rhetorical study reads "the tropes, arguments, and narratives of its object texts (whether literary or nonliterary) within their socio-political contexts of cultural production and reception."[25] The rhetoric embodied in poch@ pop culture, by its very definition, rests beneath the broader spectrum of cultural rhetoric that engages with socio-political realities. Therefore, autobiography provides another point of access for the examination of pop culture sites of analysis that compete with colonial, neocolonial, and neoliberal narratives regarding people of Latin American heritage in the U.S.

As a poch@ teaching and researching in English Studies, I have found myself in the lived contradiction where I write in English about the inherently translingual space occupied by borderlands rhetoric. At the 2013 National Council of Teachers of English (NCTE) Conference on

DOI: 10.1057/9781137498076.0005

College Composition and Communication (CCCC), I presented on a panel called "We are the .2%" with Aja Martinez and Octavio Pimentel, chaired by Jaime Armin Mejía. The point two percent in the panel's title refers to the percentage of Latin@ students who enter the educational pipeline and earn PhDs. Compared to Anglo doctoral rates of four percent, Latin@s in English Studies remain a distinct "minority" population as a fraction of a percentage across academic fields. This panel highlights the shockingly small percentage of Latin@s in English despite the increased projected population of Latin@s in the U.S.

With my Latin@ colleagues in English Studies, a perennial issue that often arises is the topic of language. The trope of poch@, or the loosely translated pejorative connotation of "cultural traitor," has painful associations for older generations of scholars because of the assumption that Latin@s who succeed in English Studies embrace Anglo culture at the cost of their heritage and culture. Spencer Herrera's (2007) *Pochoroman: The Birth of the Chicano Writer* reaffirms the persuasive power of culturally relevant writing for poch@ writers in the process of becoming artists. Herrera notes the inherent contradiction of poch@'s connotation and its implications on language:

> Despite all the cultural nuances associated with *Pocho*, the term is mostly defined by the loss of language, specifically the inability to speak Spanish fluently. Ironically, if it is language (Spanish) that Chicanos have lost, then it is language (English) that they will use to reclaim their cultural identity, voice, and history.[26]

Even as poch@s receive criticism for not knowing the colonial language of Spanish, culture endures as a powerful motivator for becoming educated. As my poch@ colleagues and I become professionals in English Studies, we learn more about our heritage culture while earning advanced degrees in English.

Rhetoric, poch@s, and media

Political rhetoric more often demonstrates epideictic rhetoric—praise without the purpose of change—when it comes to the issues affecting people of Latin American heritage. Recent ultraconservative policy of SB 1070 and HB 2281 in Arizona, which stems from and enforces colonial narratives, have created opportune moments of *kairos* that precipitate this evaluation of poch@ rhetoric. Although the struggle in Arizona

DOI: 10.1057/9781137498076.0005

could be isolated as a local issue reflecting the state's culture, these laws nonetheless possess broader implications in U.S. political rhetoric. A salient example of how Arizona's political ethos affects the rest of the country is the statistics on immigration (over)enforcement. The Obama administration appears powerless to institute immigration reform as U.S. Immigration and Customs Enforcement (ICE) announce a record number of deportations, totaling 409,849 in 2012.[27] These numbers reinforce the enduring characterization of Latin@s as criminal, or potentially "illegal" despite superficial attention paid to their growing market share or voting power. Plato's criticism of rhetoric in the *Gorgias* as flattery and not in the pursuit of truth holds logic in the context of rhetoric pandering to the "Latino Vote," as opposed to the rhetoric manifested into legislative policy that negatively impacts Latin@s in the areas of immigration and education.

As a former educator in Arizona, I recognize how students in my classes discussed and engaged with contemporary political issues at a familiar level when presented with pop culture such as the political cartoons of Lalo Alcaraz, exemplifying how many in the U.S. regard pop culture as *their* culture. Supporting my students' perspective of pop culture, Naomi Rockler provides a compelling rationale when explaining that "[i]f Americans reject critical analysis of popular culture and other media texts, they reject analysis of a significant portion of their life activity."[28] Rockler's argument has particular import for poch@ pop because the emergence of poch@ artists is significant for primary audiences who relate, and for secondary audiences who are presented with the unfamiliar issues that poch@ pop critically addresses. Pop culture provides a generative site that illuminates social constructions of identity, culture, and rhetoric when filtered through the critical lens of scholarly inquiry. Therefore, pop culture—and the many incarnations included in the broad definition—should serve as contact zones where normalized discourse, assumptions, and beliefs circulate through texts and transmit to viewers with the ostensible purpose to primarily entertain.

Thirty years ago, a book with poch@ in the title would have no doubt examined the ideology of people with Mexican heritage who do not perform or identify with their culture. As someone who rhetorically identifies as Latin@, Mexican American, Chican@, and Poch@ depending upon context, I see the purpose of this book as two-fold: first) examine how popular culture producers have embraced poch@ as a self-identifying trope, and, in doing so, challenge deficit rhetoric; second)

DOI: 10.1057/9781137498076.0005

uncover how the trope of poch@ has been misunderstood and misused, and how Pre-Columbian rhetorical traditions inform a re-envisioning of poch@ etymology, epistemology, and poch@ pop culture. This book explores the ways that subversive poch@ pop artists create critical media, while incorporating Latin American culture into pop culture artifacts that entertain as they provoke critical awareness.

Poch@ pop culture often differs from mainstream pop culture because poch@ aesthetic sensibilities are not explicitly meant to entertain or persuade audiences to purchase a given product. The "pop" of poch@ pop remains relatively consistent with "the familiar Aristotelian schema of the four-fold causes at work in handicraft or *poeisis* (material, formal, efficient, and final) [that] were applicable only to artisanal labor."[29] I employ the "pop" in popular in a relatively denotative manner. Mainly at the margins, poch@ pop circumvents capitalism's influence for which Fredric Jameson problematizes popular mass culture for the construction of "aesthetic production and linguistic invention which have their source in group life."[30] Poch@ pop is grounded in the tradition of resistant artifacts such as murals and roadside alters which are produced for the audiences who have little to no voice against the words and actions of politicians backed by corporate campaign donations. In stark contrast, poch@ pop differs greatly from capital-driven pop culture like current reality-based mass media that explicitly market a product or brand: Donald Trump's *The Apprentice*; any of the alcohol, beauty, or jewelry lines associated with Bravo's *Real Housewives* franchises; or the cadre of perfumes, clothing lines, sponsors, or appearances promoted by *Keeping up with the Kardashians*.

Poch@ audience

Similar to Plato's warning in the *Republic* that poets portray falsehoods and stir the emotions of audiences, poch@ pop producers often satirize controversies to engage with the pathos of the growing audience in the U.S. In an interview with cartoonist and *Pocho.com* editor-in-chief Lalo Alcaraz, Anabell Romero of Univision news describes the growing audience as "Pocho":

> Now more than 20 years later all media, including English-speaking stations, are scrambling to find ways of reaching that "Pocho" audience. In 2010 Census numbers came out showing that the Latino population had grown

DOI: 10.1057/9781137498076.0005

from 35.3 million to 50.5 million, accounting for more than half of the nation's population growth…As a result an unsurprisingly birth of Latino aimed news websites emerged in efforts to attract the bicultural Latino market.[31]

Romero's story on Alcaraz, "*Entendiendo la 'Pocho' life en los USA*," is indicative of the increased attention paid to the English-dominant poch@ audience in the U.S., evident by the publication of the story in both Spanish and English. Appealing to Alcaraz's poch@ fans, *Univision's* story in English further exemplifies how language continues to serve as a gate-keeping apparatus for proudly monolingual U.S. audiences. The tension associated with language in the U.S. could be attributed to the ideological belief in American exceptionalism, which assuages much of the U.S from accommodating to the rest of the world.

Reclaiming Poch@ Pop's focus on pop culture in the U.S. does not seek to perpetuate American exceptionalism by suggesting in any way that pop culture does not thrive in Latin American countries. This focus should instead be read as an indictment of the U.S. market, which rarely pays attention to non-English language cultural productions. Criticism of the U.S. and their (neo)colonial relationship with Latin American countries has come since Hernan Cortez arrived in the sixteenth century[32] and persists, notably through the 2009 Summit of the Americas when Venezuelan President Hugo Chavez presented U.S. President Barrack Obama with a copy of Eduardo Galeano's *The Open Veins of Latin America: Five Centuries of the Pillage of a Continent*. The genre of the book was appropriate for the context of the summit, in that it chronicles the interferences of the U.S. economically and politically in Central and South America.[33]

Similarly in Latin American pop culture, one of the most critically and popularly acclaimed albums of 2010, Calle 13's *Entre Los Que Quieran* dealt with themes related to the exploitation of Latin America, most notably in the song entitled "Latinoamérica." The resistant anthem includes Spanish lyrics that can loosely be translated as the female singer saying that the natural resources of the wind, sun, rain, warmth of the sun, clouds, and nature's colors cannot be bought, along with her happiness and pain. The border that language creates between Latin American perspectives and U.S. audiences greatly reduces the possibility that these critical views will crossover. Even when Calle 13's *Entre Los Que Quieran* won nine Latin Grammy awards and was nominated for a Best Latin Pop, Rock, or Urban album at the 2012 Grammys, there was very little consideration given by mainstream U.S. media to the issues raised by the album.

DOI: 10.1057/9781137498076.0005

Furthermore, the omission of Latin American pop culture perspectives in the U.S. parallels the hiring practices of mainstream U.S. pop culture producers who have a reductive view of what audiences understand and would like to see. What is facilitated by the continued use of stereotypes that constitute so-called industry shorthand is the lack of representation by people of Latin American heritage and the omission of material affecting said population in the U.S. Hector Amaya argues that this omission in the media is an alarming trend that persists despite the work of legal and media activists:

> Latino numbers in English-language media industries remain dismally low (Keller, 1994; Mayer, 2003; Noriega, 2000; Ramirez Berg, 2002; Rodriguez, 1999). Simply, Latinas/os have a hard time getting access to mainstream media jobs....In mainstream, English-speaking television, Latinos accounted for 6.5 percent of prime-time characters and 6 percent of opening credit characters in 2003 (Children Now, 2004). This is a significant improvement from 1999, when Latino prime-time representation was around 2 percent.[34]

These statistics provide logic for arguments about exclusion from the mainstream and demonstrate why poch@ pop artists must have pathos to produce as well as the ability to invent their own discursive artifacts. This data also supports the do-it-yourself (DIY) ethos that I describe later more in detail as embodied in a *rascuache* (making do with what is at hand; also *rasquache*) production methodology.

Self-identifying tropes

Rhetorical performance scholars have pointed to the turn in criticism when identity formation included the development of critical awareness of social inequality such as the intersection of rhetoric, policy, and identity. Michelle Holling illuminates the inequality in the media and relates this inequality to recent trends in rhetorical scholarship by and about Latin@s. Developing from issues related to representation, she notes, "alternate conclusions about a 'Latina/o' identity demonstrating that material exigencies and social inequities shape the identities promoted. Suggested then is the import of self-generated discursive identities as a means of asserting subjectivity and agency."[35] Generating self-identifiers is something that marginalized groups have done as a method for reclaiming agency. In response to Kenneth Burke's notion of the "master tropes,"[36] Henry Louis Gates argues that "we might think of these as

DOI: 10.1057/9781137498076.0005

the 'master's tropes,' and of Signifyin(g) as the slave's trope, the trope of tropes...a trope-reversing trope, a figure of a figure."³⁷ Gates' scholarship has political import about identity that demonstrates how tropes have the potential to resist and challenge the dominant meaning of what a trope has previously communicated. Like the once pejorative signifying monkey, poch@ has been reclaimed from its pejorative meaning to signify a metaphor of agency by the very same people it once marked as lacking.

Reclaiming Poch@ Pop contributes to the important project of highlighting the diverse media representations and productions of people of color by identifying and examining pop culture that resists rhetoric of cultural deficiency. The ethos of poch@ pop is one of resistance which negotiates cultural deficiency through subversive rhetorical productions and practices that engage with issues of immigration, identity, and education. This work focuses on the reclaimed trope of poch@ as people of Latin American heritage who are influenced by Anglo culture, which traditionally signified the negative connotation of "cultural traitor" in the Mexican dialect of Spanish. However, this book examines the pop cultural productions of artists who self-identify as poch@, including Lalo Alcaraz's *Pocho.com* and *Pocho Hour of Power* and Guillermo Gómez-Peña because of his troupe Pocha Nostra, although there are others such as *Pocho in Greater Mexico* blogger Romeo Guzman, and photographer Pocho-One. *Reclaiming Poch@ Pop* engages with rhetoric of not just resistance, but also the rhetorical elements and strategies of poch@s who negotiate the expectations of mainstream audiences, while often subverting these very same assumptions.

The cinematic representations of poch@ culture such as Ritchie Valens in *La Bamba* and Selena Quintanilla-Pérez in *Selena* provide well-known examples of pop culture that have been accepted by the mainstream while presenting Spanish-language music and the diversity of poch@ experiences in the U.S. While films such as *Selena* and *La Bamba* received mainstream acceptance, self-identifying poch@ pop producers remain subversive in their cultural productions. Some of the primary motivations for this discussion of poch@ pop stem from the responses of *Pocho.com's* editor-in-chief Lalo Alcaraz to Arizona's Senate Bill 1070 and House Bill 2281, which sanctioned racial-profiling and outlawed Mexican American Studies respectively. Even though poch@ pop embodies an emerging brand of resistant pop culture, these pop culture sites of analysis additionally reveal historical and etymological connections,

DOI: 10.1057/9781137498076.0005

specifically between poch@ and the Pre-Columbian pochteca discussed in the *Florentine Codex* of the sixteenth century. The Pre-Columbian root of poch@ prophetically possesses community-oriented characteristics and ethos that many contemporary poch@ pop producers continue to embody. In addition, the texts examined in *Poch@ Pop* engage with local policy while also satirizing transnational pop culture icons like Mickey Mouse that subsume and erase other cultures with its globalizing effect.[38]

Mesoamerican poch@ rhetoric

Depending upon the historical context, poch@ can be offensive in much the same way that many terms of endearment can become insults when uttered by an unsuitable speaker to the wrong audience for an inappropriate purpose. Remarkably, poch@ incorporates critical consciousness and a love of cultural contradictions that allows the trope to be woven into a much more elaborate tapestry of cultural and linguistic *mestizaje* (mixed-blood). Poch@ represents a growing number of the diverse populations of Latin American heritage and the epistemology stemming from Pre-Columbian Aztec and Mayan civilizations. Poch@ pop culture contributes to the struggle for equality initiated by the Chicano Civil Rights Movement and this book should be viewed in the critical genealogy of new mestiza feminist, Gloria Anzaldúa, re-imagining a trope that has yet to be appropriated by politicians and mainstream pop culture.

The growing voice of poch@ pop producers challenges prevailing assumptions transmitted through mainstream cultural productions that mischaracterize and portray people of Latin American heritage as deficient, according to the "common sense" espoused by historical narratives. Historian Emma Pérez attributes the assumptions embedded in pop culture as owing to the "stereotypes [that] serve to produce particular systems of thought."[39] These stereotypes transmit through historical misrepresentations of people of color, perpetuating deficiency rhetoric. Pérez's work informs the greater cultural significance of the pop culture covered in *Reclaiming Poch@ Pop* by defining history as a narrative constructed by colonizers to subjugate the colonized, defining historical knowledge as "the production of normative history through discursive practice."[40] If stereotypes created by those in power serve as symbols for meaning-making—given that stereotypes portray the

DOI: 10.1057/9781137498076.0005

subject as deficient[41]—then it should come as no surprise that the ideologies represented in pop cultural productions are a part of much broader hegemonic projects of subjugation. The enduring colonial nature of systemic racism, namely, is undergirded by policy that maintains racial inequality in the U.S. and promotes Anglo supremacy. The symbiotic relationship between supremacy rhetoric and ultraconservative policy ensures the subjugation of brown folk in the U.S., thereby keeping them from being hired for mainstream pop culture projects or from receiving attention from mainstream media outlets.

Pérez's framework for interpreting colonial narratives reveals embedded assumptions about poch@s in literary portrayals.[42] These discursive representations inculcate ideas forwarded in early linguistic scholarship that reaffirm oversimplified colonial standards of authenticity. Aida Hurtado and Carlos Arce regard poch@, without any qualifier, as a generational category with implications on linguistic integration and self-identification. Hurtado and Arce reductively deploy "Pocho" to label and distinguish between the different generations who self-identify as "*Mexicano*":

> Approximately 50 percent of the Pochos are naturalized citizens while only about 12 percent of *mexicanos* have U.S. citizen status…Pochos also have a high percentage of parents born in Mexico (76.6 percent of the fathers; 83.3 percent of the mothers)… Although outwardly Pochos may be most similar to Chicanos, within the family they may bear more similarity to the *mexicano*.[43]

Though the purpose of Hurtado and Arce's work is to demonstrate the linguistic diversity within Mexican American communities, their use of poch@ continues to categorize Mexican Americans within a quasi-authenticity spectrum. Unfortunately, this work does little more than re-inscribe a colonial paradigm. By their logic, those who self-identify as *Mexicano* are characterized as less Anglo than Chicanos, thus framing Chicanos as lacking an essentialized Mexican quality or characteristic. The superficially neutral scientific presentation of statistics and percentages using poch@ in this manner ignores its rhetorical power as a subversive trope that challenges the other-ing which colonial taxonomies enact and maintain.

Hurtado and Arce also reiterate how the inability to speak Spanish has served as a measure of authenticity for those identified as poch@s. The rearticulating of colonial standards often appears in discussions from outside the poch@ community, in the form of cultural deficiency

DOI: 10.1057/9781137498076.0005

rhetoric. In *Bootstraps: From an American Academic of Color,* Victor Villanueva addresses the roots of cultural deficiency theories that were prevalent among linguists who argued that the children from supposedly "deficient" cultures should be regarded as having no language.[44] English and Asian American Studies scholar, LuMing Mao, identifies the presence of deficiency rhetoric in the context of evaluating a culture's rhetorical tradition as "a 'deficiency' model—where one particular culture (read as non-Western) is determined to be lacking a concept of rhetoric or, worse still, a rhetorical tradition."[45] The cultural deficiency model, which Villanueva and Mao identify, illuminates the implied logic in arguments about Latin@s "lagging" and related discourse asserting that this population, as a monolith, does not care about education.[46] In this book, deficiency rhetoric can be understood as the underlying assumptions embedded in rhetoric, policy, and cultural productions framing brown bodies as lacking with regard to the influence of culture on citizenship, legality, and education.

The pop culture productions and producers examined in poch@ pop oppose, resist, and negotiate the cultural deficiency rhetoric that transmit stereotypes and justify unequal relationships of hegemonic power. Poch@ pop can be included in the recent scholarship that unpacks the efforts and focuses on the needs of poch@ communities;[47] specifically, these scholars unveil "the rhetorical spaces—manifesting in visual texts, the theater, and public streets—created by activists and artists to call attention to the particular struggles that have and continue to confront Latina/os."[48] *Reclaiming Poch@ Pop* builds on this scholarship by integrating Pre-Columbian rhetorical study that further supports current projects of indigeneity and social justice. Pre-Columbian literacy and history demonstrate how the history, culture, and rhetoric of poch@s are rooted in the social epistemic of the Americas.[49] By social epistemic, I refer to the connection between geographic space and knowledge created by the cultures and people who occupy those locations.

The important work of scholars Damián Baca and Victor Villanueva with Pre-Columbian and Mesoamerican traditions of literacy and knowledge provide an epistemological foundation for countering rhetoric of cultural deficiency.[50] Remarkably, the Nahuatl root "pochteca" of the contemporary poch@ appeared in the sixteenth century *Florentine Codex*; however, the lost connection has left poch@ as a floating signifier in the works of Jose Villarreal's *Pocho,* Richard Rodriguez's *Hunger of Memory,* and Gloria Anzaldúa's *Borderlands/La Frontera.* In much

DOI: 10.1057/9781137498076.0005

the same way that William Nericcio unmasks the racist simulacra of Speedy Gonzalez in *Tex[t]-Mex*[51], this book traces the etymology of poch@ to the Aztec pochteca, uncovering how the once pejorative trope should be re-imagined. In doing so, this work unpacks the rhetorical strategies which provide insight into why it has been appropriated by artists and implicitly accepted by mainstream audiences in cinematic representations.[52] *Reclaiming Poch@ Pop* illuminates the historical trajectory of poch@ subversion in the Americas, thereby tracing the roots of a generative trope for the next generation of self-identifying poch@ popular culture producers and consumers. This is especially imperative because of the overtly discriminatory legislation in states like Arizona, Alabama, and Texas that call into question the legitimacy of citizenship and knowledge for brown bodies.

Summary of chapters

Including this introductory preface, *Reclaiming Poch@ Pop* is comprised of five chapters that begin with cinematic pop culture that I identify as proto-poch@ pop. Following an examination of proto-poch@ pop films *La Bamba* and *Selena* as well as poch@ pop artist Robert Rodriguez, I then outline the theory and methods framing *Reclaiming Poch@ Pop* in Chapter 2. In Chapter 3, I look at Lalo Alcaraz's work that engages in a subversive dialogue with the ultraconservative policy in Arizona. I move backwards through time in Chapter 4, vis-à-vis the collaborative work of Guillermo Gómez-Peña, to the etymological root of poch@. The examination of the trajectory of poch@ from the Pre-Columbian era exposes rhetorical elements that contribute to the contemporary appropriation of poch@, as discussed in Chapter 5. By uncovering the Nahuatl root of poch@, this book contributes to the growing body of work in Pre-Columbian Rhetoric[53] while engaging with scholarship that examines popular culture through the interconnections between cultural rhetoric and Latin American Studies.

Chapter 2 examines the positive representations of proto-poch@ pop artists Ritchie Valens and Selena Quintanilla-Pérez, framed in a discussion of poch@ pop artist Robert Rodriguez. I focus on *La Bamba* and *Selena* because they represent the lives and music of poch@s in the U.S. who are English-dominant and achieve mainstream acceptance, while performing Spanish-language music. These films could be considered a

DOI: 10.1057/9781137498076.0005

part of what was discussed as the "Hispanic Hollywood" in the *Bronze Screen*[54]; however, more importantly, these films mark a break from the culturally deficient representations of Latin@s as banditos or exoticized, sexual Other that persist.[55] This examination of proto-poch@ films sets the foundation for further discussion of the poch@ trope and identity that challenge negative portrayals in mainstream representations of Latin@ language and culture.

In Chapter 3, I outline the theoretical and methodological framework that explains the resistance to colonial narratives that subjugate Latin@s in the U.S. and frame them as culturally deficient according to colonial standards.[56] Emma Pérez's notion of the decolonial imaginary provides a framework for how artists reveal the possibilities for resistance outside of dominant colonial narratives.[57] In addition, the *rascuache* methodology that Guillermo Gómez-Peña[58] outlines reveals how the use of the pejorative term poch@ serves as an appropriation that challenges deficiency-based colonial narratives. Gómez-Peña resists deficit rhetoric by re-claiming the trope of poch@ and by challenging the outdated colonial binary paradigm, evidenced by the naming of his troupe La Pocha Nostra and incorporating a character by the telling name of Pocho-Dos.

In Chapter 4, I discuss the growing population of poch@s in the U.S., and mainstream integration of poch@s such as the introduction of Al Madrigal on the *Daily Show* to ultimately focus on selected political cartoons of Lalo Alcaraz. Again, Pérez's decolonial imaginary illuminates how pop culture producers subvert dominant colonial narratives that tokenize people of color in the media or exoticize in political rhetoric. Further, this chapter specifically looks at how the art of Pocho.com's Lalo Alcaraz resists cultural deficit rhetoric by challenging policy framing all Latin@s as potentially "illegal" (SB 1070), and racist in their education (HB 2281). In consideration of the growing poch@ population, Alcaraz's art demonstrates the kinds of subversive messages that appeal to the growing population of cultural producers and consumers.

Chapter 5 traces the etymological connection between poch@ and pochteca[59], examining the traveling merchant role of the pochteca that crossed territories and spoke in the tongue of the foreign territory. The historical origin of poch@ reveals salient connections for the contemporary reclamation by poch@ pop artists. As the site of analysis, Gómez-Peña's collaboration of the *Codex Espangliensis* provides a generative visual performance of Mesoamerican literacy practices, thereby showing how the integration of historical tropes resists colonial rhetoric about

DOI: 10.1057/9781137498076.0005

Latin@s in popular culture.[60] Gómez-Peña's visually-oriented text brings the conversation full circle by looking at comic-like representations that critically juxtapose mainstream pop culture icons like Mickey Mouse with images from the conquest of the Americas.

Conclusion

On the occasions when I have been invited to speak about pedagogy, I cannot escape the influence of poch@ pop when explaining my teaching persona. I explain that while many of my colleagues no doubt image themselves as Robin Williams in *Dead Poets Society* (1989), I instead envision Edward James Olmos' Jaime Escalante in *Stand and Deliver* (1988). Addressing the concern of classroom management, I use Olmos' Escalante as an example of a playful persona, acting out Olmos' "finger man" monologue of multiplying by nine using his fingers to demonstrate a practical mathematics technique while deflecting the aggression of a student. I'm not always sure how many of the Anglo teachers, to whom I am presenting, are familiar with *Stand and Deliver*, but the "finger man" provides an embodied performance that connects with the abstract pedagogical persona. Many of the rhetorical productions that make up the body of texts discussed in *Reclaiming Poch@ Pop* do appear in part because of their pedagogical and presentation efficacy. The power of pop culture to inspire responses—whether shocked, confused, or amused—speaks to the motivation for many educators to connect with students by reflecting what the students see as their culture back to them.

Notes

1   Cabrera, Milem and Marx 2012, 1–19.
2   Tatum 2001, 54.
3   Villanueva 1993.
4   Passel and Cohn 2008.
5   Acuña 2013.
6   Anzaldúa 1987; Rodriguez 1982; Villarreal 1959.
7   Baca 2008; Soto 2010.
8   Lunsford and Ouzgane 2004.
9   Hugo-Lopez 2013.
10 Hugo-Lopez 2013, 18.

DOI: 10.1057/9781137498076.0005

11   Gates 1988.

12   Burke 1969.

13   Anzaldúa 1987; Rodriguez 1982; Villarreal 1959.

14   I define *latinidad* as the performance of "Latino-ness," either through language or through other symbolic action.

15   Aldama 2009.

16   Villanueva 1993.

17   Pérez 1999.

18   Olmos 1997.

19   Rodriguez 1997, 284.

20   Plato 1978.

21   Hernández 1991, 20.

22   Villanueva 1993, xviii.

23   Hesford 1999.

24   Hesford 1999, 4.

25   Mailloux qtd. in Hesford, 1999, 4.

26   Herrera 2007, vii–viii.

27   "FY 2012: ICE announces year-end removal numbers, highlights focus on key priorities and issues new national detainer guidance to further focus resources." News Releases. Immigration and Customs Enforcement. 21. Dec. 2012. 18 Aug. 2013. http://www.ice.gov/news/releases/1212/121221washington dc2.htm.

28   Rockler 2002, 98.

29   Jameson 1979, 131.

30   Jameson 1979, 140.

31   Romero 2013.

32   See *The Broken Spears* (1962) by Miguel León Portilla.

33   The *Huffington Post's* "Chavez Gives Obama a History Book" quotes the Associated Press's reporting of Venezuelan President Chavez presenting U.S. President Obama with *The Open Veins of Latin America* in front of photographers. http://www.huffingtonpost.com/2009/04/18/chavez-gives-obama-a-book_n_188582.html May 9, 2009;s updated May 25, 2011.

34   Amaya 2010, 806.

35   Holling 2008, 304.

36   Burke 1969.

37   Gates 1988, 52.

38   Alcaraz 2004; Gómez-Peña, Chagoya and Rice 2000.

39   Pérez 1999, 12.

40   Pérez 1999, 7.

41   Steele 2010.

42   Anzaldúa 1987; Rodriguez 1982; Villarreal 1959.

43   Hurtado and Arce 1986, 114–115.

DOI: 10.1057/9781137498076.0005

44 Villanueva 1993, 10.
45 Mao 2003, 401.
46 Valenzuela 1999.
47 Calafell and Delgado 2004; Cintron 1997; Enck-Wanzer 2006; Holling and Calafell 2007; Licona 2012.
48 Holling 2008, 304–305
49 Berlin 1988.
50 Baca and Villanueva 2010.
51 Nericcio 2007.
52 *Pocho Handbook* 1980; Townsend 2000.
53 Baca 2008; Baca and Villanueva 2010.
54 Fregoso 1993.
55 Mauricio 2007; Yosso 2002.
56 Bhabha 1994.
57 Pérez 1999.
58 Gómez-Peña 2000.
59 *Pocho Handbook* 1980; Townsend 2000.
60 Baca 2008.

DOI: 10.1057/9781137498076.0005

2
Proto-Poch@ Representations in Film: Exploitation or Bust

Abstract: *Chapter 2 examines the positive representations of proto-poch@ pop artists Ritchie Valens and Selena Quintanilla-Pérez, framed in a discussion of poch@ pop filmmaker Robert Rodriguez. This chapter focuses on proto-poch@ films* La Bamba *and* Selena *because they represent the lives and music of poch@s in the U.S. who are English-dominant and achieve mainstream acceptance, while performing Spanish-language music. This examination of proto-poch@ films sets the foundation for further discussion of the poch@ trope and identity that challenge negative portrayals in mainstream representations of Latin@ language and culture.*

Medina, Cruz. *Reclaiming Poch@ Pop: Examining the Rhetoric of Cultural Deficiency.* New York: Palgrave Macmillan, 2015. DOI: 10.1057/9781137498076.0006.

DOI: 10.1057/9781137498076.0006

During elementary school, I went with my family to see both *La Bamba* (1987) and *Stand and Deliver* (1988), twice respectively in theaters. My Chicano father grew up playing guitar in the sixties, was the first in his family to attend college, and subsequently taught English; so he no doubt returned for second showings—with my mother, brother and me in tow—because he saw his bi-cultural experiences positively reflected in these films. It was not a point of contention that Edward James Olmos' portrayal of Jaime Escalante in *Stand and Deliver* focused on teaching Latin@ students to pass a standardized Advanced Placement test, despite the inherent racial bias of standardized tests.[1] As filmgoers, my family harbored no resentment because Filipino American Lou Diamond Phillips portrayed the young Chicano, Richard Valenzuela, or that Valenzuela's name was anglicized to Ritchie Valens. These films mirrored my father's experiences—and no doubt those experiences of many in his generation—while also achieving acceptance by mainstream audiences. The Mexican, Mexican American, and Hispanic cultural identities, traditions, and messages transmitted through these cinematic productions familiarized Anglo audiences with less stereotypical representations of the poch@ experience in the U.S. than previously depicted.

Films of this cinematic era fall into what has been called the "Hispanic Hollywood" category because of their mainstream crossover and absence of overt opposition to racism and societal oppression as in Chicano cinema like *Raices de Sangre* (1977), *Alambrista* (1979), and *Seguín* (1981).[2] Despite being some of my favorite representations of poch@s in film from my childhood, these pieces of pop culture adhere to familiar structures and values of Hollywood productions that restrict and suppress explicit messages of subversion and resistance. But the right amount of tension between overt resistance and commercial success is not easily achieved. During an interview with Feliciano Garcia about *Machete Kills* (2013), poch@ filmmaker Robert Rodriguez was asked if he was trying to send a message or create an underlying tone in his B-movie homage *Machete* (2010) and the sequel *Machete Kills* (2013). In his response, Rodriguez admits to producing an "action hero popcorn flick" while encoding a socially conscious message:

> [I]n the 70s [there] were filmmakers who had a message that they wanted to get across, but the only person who would give them the job were these exploitation studios that would say 'say whatever you want, but there's got to be violence, there's got to be action, there's got to be comedy—you got to get butts in seats.' So I like that juxtaposition of ideologies and…that it has

DOI: 10.1057/9781137498076.0006

to be big, it has to be crazy, it has to be larger than life, sexy women, explosions, action, but a social message that I trying—the filmmaker side of Robert Rodriguez is trying—to get some social goodness in there as well.[3]

Rodriguez's explanation for the need to veil his political commentary with exaggerated cinematic violence provides a useful context for distinguishing between what was possible in exploitation films and those films backed by mainstream Hollywood infrastructure. Because of the necessity to "get butts in seats" decades after the exploitation era, Rodriguez's films continue to communicate messages of "social goodness" amid highly-stylized violence and highly-sexualized female representations. Although films such as *La Bamba, Stand and Deliver*, and *Selena* do not voice direct opposition to the subjugation of Latinas and Latinos as films such as *Machete*, this chapter examines films that possess proto-poch@ pop characteristics. Unlike the poch@ pop that performs rhetorical strategies of what I term subversive complicity[4]—working within a system while working against it and resisting cultural deficiency rhetoric—the cinematic productions of the mid-eighties and nineties disrupt the silencing of Latin@s in mainstream pop culture, while providing cinematic role models for this current generation of poch@ pop producers.

Rhetorically, the success of poch@ pop to persuade mainstream audiences can occur due to the numerous appeals, genres, and the opportune moment of *kairos*. In addition, historical context should not be discounted when considering the rhetorical efficacy of these cultural productions. Between the release of *La Bamba* and *Selena*, the market for Latin@ consumers doubled in size, no doubt in part because of the shift in pop culture productions. Because cinematic pop culture is intertwined with show business, or "the business of show," analysis of the work of communication scholars and their audience provide important statistical data to support the aforementioned shifts in Latin@ pop culture productions. Market analyst América Rodriguez describes the increased buying power of Latin@s when explaining that "the amount of goods and services purchased by U.S. Latinos has roughly doubled from 1986 to 1996, and now stands at 223 billion dollars (Douglas, 1996). These numbers are promoted by the marketers of U.S. Latino media firms, and are a staple of the industry trade press."[5] I do not seek to prove causation between the growing size of the Latin@ audience and the embracement of the trope of poch@ by poch@ pop producers. However, the increase

DOI: 10.1057/9781137498076.0006

in audience size offers greater context of the rhetorical situation, thereby demonstrating why the influence of poch@ pop producers can cross, at times, into the mainstream.

Even though pop culture can serve as a resource and site of resistance and negotiation, early poch@ pop productions draw less complex depictions of Latin American culture. The proto-poch@ pop I discuss tends to downplay explicit resistance to Anglo assimilation and erasure of culture. Still, they successfully normalize the presence of brown bodies as cinematic protagonists, as well as poch@ experiences, language, history, and music for non-Latin@ audiences. Simultaneously, proto-poch@ pop films reflect the worldviews, desires, and marginalized experiences of poch@ audiences. Before it was possible for current poch@ pop producers such as Robert Rodriguez, Lalo Alcaraz, Al Madrigal, and Guillermo Gómez-Peña to openly contest rhetoric of cultural deficiency misrepresenting Latin@s for mainstream audiences, proto-poch@ pop artists had to paint cultural depictions with much broader brushes that could not detail the complexity and diversity of experiences in the U.S.

Bronze screens in Hispanic Hollywood

Despite Latin@ pop culture scholars having dubbed the era of films such as *La Bamba* and *Selena* as "Hispanic Hollywood,"[6] the positive messages about identity more closely align with Chican@ consciousness, rather than the ethos of the Nixon-era trope of Hispanic. The films discussed below as proto-poch@ films "combine Chicano expertise—and sometimes control—with Hollywood production values and distribution. These filmic productions are more closely affiliated with Chicano independent films than with the average Hollywood production that makes use of Chicano material."[7] That the material in both *Selena* and *La Bamba* draws from the biographies of musicians Selena Quintanilla-Pérez and Ritchie Valenzuela shows the persuasive power of pop and rock en Español (Spanish language rock and roll) as genres of pop culture that communicate the bi-cultural experience of poch@s in the U.S. Additionally, the genre of the biopic establishes credibility and appeals the pathos of audiences who identify with the universal themes of family, music, and love in spite of the unique poch@ experiences.

Previous attention paid to *La Bamba* and *Selena* focused on issues such as reinforced constructed binaries, negative representations of gender,

DOI: 10.1057/9781137498076.0006

and criticisms of patriarchy.[8] This chapter, however, contributes to the growing discussions of the positive shift in aesthetic representations, feminist performance and iconography that these films provide.[9] This work follows the roots laid by Gloria Anzaldúa's theories on mestiza identity and consciousness construction in the U.S.-Mexico borderlands, and Latin@ rhetoric and epistemology that continue to negotiate and grapple with the complex issue of identity.[10] Similarly, the rhetoric of Latin@ pop culture examines nuances and sites to further unravel internalized constructs of identity, as well as the externalized forces in the form of contemporary policy shaping the societal perceptions of Latin@ identity in the U.S. Representations of identity in pop culture serve as models, presenting the archetypes that become the cultural touchstones in what has become a pop culture-centric generation of consumers. Identifying these films as proto-poch@ pop cinematic productions, I highlight the aspects of pop culture that illuminate the colonizing effect of media misrepresentations, and resist, challenge, contest, and, at the very least, complicate narratives portraying Latin@s as culturally deficient.

Michelle Holling describes the proto-poch@ pop era in the medium of letters as a historical moment characterized by prevailing racism and sexism. She explains that the literary mode was denied Latin@s by "underlying racism and sexism along with gatekeeping efforts by publishers, compounded by perceptions that Chicana/o books may not appeal to a broader (read: mainstream) audience."[11] While the primary concern of this book is with the rhetoric communicated in the pop culture by poch@ producers and for poch@s consumers, the issue of distribution supplies historical context about hegemonic systems that silence Latin@ voices, especially explicitly oppositional voices in pop culture. Ideological boundaries are drawn by the self-identifying tropes of Chican@, Mexican-American, and poch@ in much the same way that the labeling of films such as *Zoot Suit* (1981) and *La Bamba* (1986) as "Hispanic Hollywood" problematizes the rhetorical power of these productions when compared to so-called "Chicano Films" like *Raíces de Sangre* (1977), *El Mariachi* (1993), and *Selena* (1997).[12] While the productions I identify as poch@ pop seemingly reinstate a different taxonomy that could be criticized as simply another step in an ideological continuum, I posit that poch@ pop productions provoke critical consciousness by communicating critical messages encoded in pop culture concerned with entertainment value.

DOI: 10.1057/9781137498076.0006

Spectacles of classroom violence

Unfortunately, violence in and out of the classroom is the expectation of many film-going audiences in part because of the production of films like *Dangerous Minds* (1997), *187* (1997), and *The Substitute* (1996) that perpetuate deficiency rhetoric about students of color.[13] In those films, brown students are portrayed as thugs, gangbangers, and highly-sexualized, which harkens back to familiar tropes of B-movies and westerns in "Old Mexico." The pop cultural productions discussed below reflect Gary Keller's point that "Chicano filmmakers have produced films that subvert the stock genres and formulas that Hollywood has used for decades in making Western, 'bad Mexican' or greaser, and border immigration films and musicals."[14] Although Keller uses the term "Chicano" to characterize the filmmakers who subvert dominant cinematic narratives, the films I describe as proto-poch@ pop address issues such as language and identity that are closely associated with the trope of poch@ and Chican@ sensibilities. Importantly, the scholarship and cultural productions I discuss demonstrate a particular trajectory in Latin@ criticism over the past two decades.

Admittedly, this section merely skims the surface of films that I identify as proto-poch@ pop. Still, the films and lenses for interpretation that I touch on are intentionally not meant to be an exhaustive review of the many films and volumes of scholarship dedicated to the critical examination of Latin@s in film. Instead, what follows serves as a kind of illumination, or tracing of the roots, which bear the fruit of poch@ pop; to extend the metaphor, the representations I touch on are but some of the proto-poch@ seeds—which now given the necessary time—reveal the inspiration for subversive pop culture in a historical moment where there is space for these resistant representations to mature. Despite the oppressive media representations and policy perpetuating cultural deficiency that stoke fears about the growing Latin@ population, poch@ pop rises up through the elements for critical audiences to discover in a vapid wasteland of ephemeral spectacles. Discussing the absurdity of professional wrestling, Roland Barthes describes uncritical forms of entertainment as spectacle: "[t]he public is completely uninterested in knowing whether the contest is rigged or not...the primary virtue [is] the spectacle, which is to abolish all motives and all consequences: what matters is not what it thinks but what it sees."[15] One could hardly contest Barthes' assertion vis-à-vis the mainstream success of pop culture

DOI: 10.1057/9781137498076.0006

phenomena such as *Here Comes Honey Boo-Boo, Keeping up with the Kardashians, Real Housewives of Orange County,* and *Duck Dynasty.* This is why poch@ pop is so important.

In the following section, I return again and again to Rosa Linda Fregoso's *Bronze Screen.* As a text, it embodies many of the concerns raised about this era of Hispanic Hollywood. Some of the counterpoints I make about proto-poch@ pop come as a Socratic dialogue across time and space, informing this critical undertaking on the rhetorical efficacy of pop culture. My own fondness for the films I identify as proto-poch@ pop follows the nostalgia that Fregoso identifies as a component of Hispanic Hollywood's constructed representation, which made these films well-received despite some of the cliché tropes they include. Applicable to beloved films like *Zoot Suit, La Bamba, Stand and Deliver,* and *Selena* that receive criticism for their portrayals of crime, silenced resistance, patriarchy and the sexualization of Latina bodies, Luz Calvo accounts for the consumption of deficiency rhetoric encoded in these films. She recognizes what she describes as "the coexistence of contradictory feelings and attitudes toward one [media] object" as "ambivalence" to potential stereotypical representations so long as they connect in some way with the cultural memory or reflect experiences of the audience.[16]

Calvo's discussion of ambivalence is supported by the agendas encoded in the messages of pop productions. In a salient example, Selma Hayek's role in *From Dusk Till Dawn* (1996) as a scantily-clad biker bar dancer reinforces highly-sexualized media representations of Latinas. Robert Rodriguez explains Hayek's role as strategic subversion within an existing narrative:

> [P]eople can go, "Oh look, it's the same thing, it's Latina women being stereotyped." I guess they could see it that way. I based it on the requirements of the script that Quentin [Tarantino] had written, and I just sort of changed it a little bit to make it more based in Mexican history. And more about the women.[17]

The contradictory feelings, which Calvo notes, are validated given the familiar cinematic tropes; however, Rodriguez performs subversive complicity as he works within a dominant system while challenging it by imbuing it with culturally relevant material. Although Quentin Tarantino hardly represents hegemony, his cinematic tributes to the exploitation genre—to which Tarantino pays homage in his cinematic oeuvre— uncritically reproduce racist and sexist representations. Rodriguez complicates Hayek's image as an exotic dancer with the presence of her

DOI: 10.1057/9781137498076.0006

snake, which alludes to Coatlicue the Earth Mother: "Come, little green snake. Let the wound caused by the serpent be cured by the serpent."[18] Anzaldúa's description of the Coatlicue state as material and celestial helps to explain the duality of Hayek's highly-sexualized image with the history and culture she represents: "the mountain, the Earth Mother who conceived all celestial beings…duality in life, a synthesis of duality, and a third perspective."[19] In the same interview, Rodriguez explains that Hayek's character fulfills a *reconquista* (re-conquest) revenge narrative, killing off the Anglo motorcycle riders as an unstoppable mestiza demigoddess.

As a fourth wall-breaking supernatural being, Edward James Olmos's iconic performance of the *pachuco* in Luis Valdez's *Zoot Suit* (1981) walks a similarly thin line between gangbanger stereotype and demigod of Chican@ resistance. Olmos's pachuco jars the viewer by breaking with convention with his post-modern interaction with the audience within the film. Valdez's pachuco creation both takes part in and disrupts the narrative *mes-en-scène*, drawing attention to the artifice of the narrative. In support of its pop culture significance, film scholars note how *Zoot Suit* pushes "the boundaries of conventional narrative discourse."[20] Fregoso attests to the proto-poch@ pop qualities via the recognition of Valdez's pairing of experimentation with an enduring symbol of political opposition. Fregoso explains Valdez's subversion while negotiating the Hollywood industry:

> *Zoot Suit* imbues dominant cinematic codes with those from an oppositional cultural tradition, continuing in the intertextual tradition of the early period of Chicano filmmaking…the production of the film within the mainstream Hollywood industry underlines the logic of dominant hegemonic incorporation of oppositional discourses: for various historical circumstances, a corporate marketing strategy converged with a Chicano cultural politics of contestation.[21]

Considering the challenge of producing a mainstream film with a counter-hegemonic message, the production and distribution of *Zoot Suit* was a feat. To return briefly to Barthes' description of professional wrestling as spectacle, the deconstruction of cinematic narrative in *Zoot Suit* creates a theatrical spectacle for mainstream audiences less interested in the themes and subject matter. The post-modern manipulation of cinematic storytelling allows Valdez to focus primarily on the logic of the oppositional discourse, resonating with audiences initially amused by the dialogic asides.

DOI: 10.1057/9781137498076.0006

Unfortunately, *Zoot Suit* serves as more of an exception rather than cinematic archetype for successful poch@ films, despite the proto-poch@ pop qualities of working within the Hollywood system while challenging the messages it proliferates. Although it would be naïve to assert that *Zoot Suit* widely changed perceptions of Latin@s, it's presence can be charted into the historical trajectory that made future poch@ productions possible. Along temporal lines, Holling identifies an ideological shift in Latin@ communities around the time of *Stand and Deliver*, moving from an ideology of silence to one of participation. Paying attention to the interplay of media and cultural relevance, Holling notes that,

> Utilized by dee-jays of a local bilingual radio station, the ideology draws upon culturally specific symbolic phrases to encourage participatory behaviors among all community members, both Mexican American and Anglo. In so doing, the ideology rhetorically intervenes in the "silence" thereby ameliorating an undesired intercultural distance between communities.[22]

The participatory behavioral shift that Holling highlights colors the reading of a film like *Stand and Deliver* that has been criticized for "diluting" historical context or supporting portrayals of Chican@s as passive agents in issues such as education. Historical context in film is by its very nature diluted by the temporal parameters of the genre.

The depiction of Jaime Escalante's professional career, however, demonstrates the participatory turn in which everyday citizens mobilized students to challenge the deficiency rhetoric in stereotypes about Latin@s and education. The real-life Escalante and his students challenged the assumptions about Latin@s through the complicit act of improving the scores of standardized test-taking. In contrast to Holling's characterization of *Stand and Deliver* as inspiring participation, poch@ pop artist Robert Rodriguez uses the film to explain why his political messages are less overt:

> I remember hearing Edward James Olmos saying how he was disappointed because he'd made *Stand and Deliver* and no Latinos showed up to watch it. And I thought to myself, 'I'm just not going to go down that road'...As soon as you feel like you're a crusader on a mission, you'll get lost. You're doing it for the wrong reasons.[23]

Rodriguez challenges the characterization of *Stand and Deliver*'s audience as participatory, although my own experience differs from Olmos' perception mediated through Rodriguez's memory. The participatory movement that Holling describes, however, contributes to a more

DOI: 10.1057/9781137498076.0006

complex understanding of the historical moment when proto-poch@ pop such as *Stand and Deliver* informed poch@ pop producers like Rodriguez.

'Fiery' Latinas

As a perennial issue in pop culture, the rhetorical construction of Latinas in film is problematic and complicated, especially with regard to cinematic constructions of identity, sexuality, and the body. The representation of Latin@ bodies in U.S. pop culture has been fraught with the erasure of Latin@ ethnicity, the exotification of sexuality, and other socially constructed mediations through which U.S. audiences have consumed Latin@ representations. Dating back to Mexican American actress Rita Hayworth, who changed her name from Margarita Carmen Cansino, crossing-over into mainstream media has meant conforming to white standards of beauty. In William Nericcio's no nonsense criticism of Hayworth's transformation, he posits:

> Rita Cansino got screwed both figuratively and literally, and the way this screwing 'functions' speaks eloquently to ethnicity and gender as lived and living categories; further, it sheds light on the way these categories have been impacted upon by motion picture technologies in the twentieth century.[24]

Nericcio holds Rita Hayworth accountable, referring to her as a "proto-Richard Rodriguez." Tragically, in the introduction of Rodriguez's work that champions assimilation, he begins by commenting derogatorily on his indigenous features: "Dark-skinned...Exotic in a tuxedo. My face is drawn to severe Indian features which would pass notice on the pages of a *National Geographic*."[25] That this internalized mindset has a historical tradition shows how intertwined notions of identity can be shaped over time by messages framing Latin@s as visually unpleasing and therefore unfit for media and pop culture representations. Again, with the film *Stand and Deliver* in mind, the legacy is even more salient given the prevalent narratives against Latin@s in the areas of both film and education.

The "fiery" modifier, like the classroom violence subtitle above, is tongue-in-cheek and plays on popular cultural narratives that transmit so-called positive representations about Latin@s, who are often praised for exoticized physical features, while ultimately constructing the Latin@

DOI: 10.1057/9781137498076.0006

body as "Other." In *The Hollywood Latina Body as Site of Social Struggle: Media Constructions of Stardom and Jennifer Lopez's 'Cross-over Butt'*, Mary Beltran addresses the media's role in the exotification of Latina bodies while using Jennifer Lopez as an example of a non-traditional beauty that challenges societal standards of beauty with her crossover success. Beltran explains that she interprets,

> Jennifer Lopez not as another victim constructed in a still-racist society as an ethnic sexual object...but as empowered and empowering through asserting qualities such as intelligence, assertiveness, and power—while also proudly displaying her non-normative body and declaring it beautiful.[26]

Lopez's ability to crossover while shifting paradigms of aesthetics accepted by mainstream audiences demonstrates the negotiation that surpasses a resistance-only approach. Unlike my tongue-in-cheek use of fiery, Beltran views Lopez as channeling this energy. In agreement with Beltran's description of Lopez's empowering presence, I recognize *Selena* as a part of the proto-poch@ pop productions that garnered mainstream attention from audiences while addressing Latin@ culture and identity in the U.S.

Looking at both *Frida* and *Selena*, Isabel Molina Guzmán, and Angharad N. Valdivia (2004) examine the representations of Hayek, Kahlo, and Lopez to analyze the gendered and racialized symbols surrounding Latinidad, as well as what they posit as Latina iconicity. Seeking to unsettle fixed notions of identity and ethnicity, Guzmán and Valdivia look at "the commodification of ethnic authenticity" and theorize that "Latina iconicity connects to broader transformative notions of transnational identities in order to problematize Western gendered and racialized narratives of ethnicity."[27] On her own, Guzmán returns to *Frida* as a site of analysis for examining ethnic identity. Guzmán examines the performance of Latina identity in the film *Frida* to demonstrate the complexity of interethnic Latina representations. Highlighting the diversity of Latin@ identities, Guzmán points out that "[t]he interethnic backgrounds of both Hayek and Kahlo problematize dominant constructions of ethnic, racial, and national identity as fixed and stable."[28] Lopez's portrayal of *Selena* similarly brings up similar issues of ethnic erasure due to Lopez's Puerto Rican heritage and Selena Quintanilla's Mexican heritage.

In the last 20 years, criticism has continued to critically analyze cultural representations while also identifying the empowering aspects

DOI: 10.1057/9781137498076.0006

of identity performance. For example, Jillian M. Báez includes *Selena* (1997) with the films *Girlfight* (2000) and *Real Women Have Curves* (2002) as embodying a *Latinidad feminista* that disrupts historical representations of Latinas in U.S. cinema.[29] Báez applauds these films for their ability to create complex and fluid Latina subjectivities that break from previous stereotypical media representations. This is perhaps one of the reasons why *Reclaiming Poch@ Pop* continues the work of examining sites and transformative tropes that negotiate transnational pop culture, which subsume cultural identifiers and re-inscribe narratives of cultural deficiency.

Se necessita un poco de gracia

Biographical films, or biopics, about musicians have the added multimedia capability of transmitting not just the life and cultural experiences of a person, but also create spaces for emotional connections to the music associated with the subject's story. Focusing the poch@ interpretive lens on the film *La Bamba*, I return to the career-altering moment when Valens met his manager. The Anglo man introduces himself by code-switching into Spanish, "My name is Bob Keene. I'm president of Del-Fi Records in Hollywood. "*¿Podemos hablar?*" Valens responds, "I don't speak Spanish."[30] For Anglo viewers, this response by Valens on one level challenged the assumption that "all Hispanics *eh-spic* Spanish." For poch@s who grew up in the U.S. speaking primarily English and experiencing rejection for not speaking Spanish, this admission by Valens symbolized a positive representation of a poch@ with Mexican heritage, who does not speak Spanish. In a single utterance, Valdez's cinematic construction of Valens confronts the implication that non-Spanish speaking poch@s have turned their backs on their culture.[31] During the historical moment when *La Bamba* was produced, the issue of not speaking the Spanish language characterizes the stigmatizing aspect of the poch@ identify, especially for those who sensed and experienced rejection from within their communities. Richard Rodriguez and Gloria Anzaldúa characterize the periods of their youth as the time when poch@ possessed its most negative meaning, capturing these moments during the same period as Valdez in *La Bamba*. Divergently, the reclamation of poch@ by contemporary pop culture producers follows more in line with Anzaldúa's new mestiza consciousness, which breaks from colonial binaries of identity, rather than Rodriguez's espousal of colonial assimilation rhetoric.

DOI: 10.1057/9781137498076.0006

While the mainstream popularity of *La Bamba* could be derided as a neoliberal celebration of Hispanic culture, the film depicts the result of the post World War II baby-boom when many Mexican American soldiers returned home and named their children Anglo names. Like brothers Ritchie and Bob in *La Bamba*, many in that generation were caught in a moment when a generation who had served the U.S. wanted to assimilate in order to avoid being treated as second-class citizens.[32] I would posit that my own grandfather and others of his generation are by default conservatively patriotic because they remain appreciative of the rights afforded to them for their service after World War II. The audiences of my father's generation were similarly willing to ignore the strategic essentialism in films such as *La Bamba* because it was the most attractive alternative for viewing productions by Latin@s. Holling accurately describes this period:

> [Full of] contradictions and failed realities for Latina/os in which cultural tensions were underway regarding affirmative action and English-only laws, increasing imbalanced political and economic status amongst Latina/os, and access to commercially successful films in Hollywood that appeared predicated upon a film's embrace of strategies of accommodation and/or assimilation.[33]

That *La Bamba* was produced during Reagan-era neoconservative policy and neoliberal assimilation rhetoric provides complicated historical context for interpreting poch@ pop. These very same tensions continue—in political theater and the execution of dehumanizing policy—thereby serving as inspiration for contemporary pop culture producers.

La Bamba further complicates the reductive colonial binary of *either* assimilation *or* cultural authenticity with regard to language given that Valens draws inspiration from a trip to Mexico. Valens only achieves his greatest success, which births the musical genre of rock en Español, by incorporating his cultural heritage into his musical career. He does so by re-envisioning the traditional *son jarocho* folk song "La Bamba" with his rock-and-roll style. In a performance of strategic essentialism, Valdez crafts a narrative in which Lou Diamond Phillips as Valens accompanies Esai Morales as Ritchie's brother Bob to a Tijuana brothel while inebriated. Still carrying his guitar at the brothel, Valens strums in accompaniment with a Mariachi band playing a folk version of "La Bamba," portrayed by real-life Chican@ rock and roll group Los Lobos. This scene marks the turning point where Valens is able to integrate his cultural heritage into a rock and roll song that becomes a breakthrough

DOI: 10.1057/9781137498076.0006

hit. Challenging the validity of Valdez's adaptation of Valens's biography, Fregoso posits that, "[t]he liberties taken by Valdez to give Valens mainstream appeal…distorted key details about Valens's childhood formation in Mexican music, depicting him instead as just a rock-and-roll musician."[34] While Valdez may have altered Valens' connection with traditional Mexican music, the incorporation of culturally relevant pop culture by a poch@ remains an important aspect of the film, inserted as a rhetorical moment of invention within the narrative. For audiences, the strategic placement of Valens's encounter with the song "La Bamba" during the second act plays into essentialized romantic views of Mexico, fulfilling expectations of mainstream audiences. At the same time, the distortion of Valens' biography allows the viewer to accompany Valens as voyeur while he experiences a cultural awakening that is linked through narrative to both his coming into sexual and indigenous spiritual consciousness. What should be taken away from *La Bamba* as a proto-poch@ pop production is how Valdez's film embodies the culturally relevant popular media that Valens produces, despite having been even perceived as a cultural traitor by those who are quick to defend colonial borders of identity.

Reinforcing the notion of identity as a socially-constructed border, Jose Manuel Valenzuela-Arce categorizes the trope of poch@ as a stereotype of Chican@ representation. In keeping with its colonial definition, Valenzuela-Arce notes that poch@ has continued to be used in Mexico to describe the degradation of the Spanish language. In *Fronteras y Representaciones Sociales: La Figura del Pocho Como Estereotipo del Chicano*, Valenzuela-Arce states that the poch@ is stereotypically portrayed as the Americanized/Anglicized person of Mexican origin who turns his or her back on tradition and does not want to take part in Mexican culture. In Mexico, the discourse about poch@ is framed by a nationalist logic: "*los pochos como que no quieren ser mexicanos* [the pochos do not want to be Mexican]."[35] Illustrating how the colonial language of Spanish is deeply intertwined in the rhetoric of what it means to be perceived well, Valenzuela-Arce echoes the Commission for the Defense of the Spanish Language and their use of the phrase "*habla bien, no te apoches* [speak well, don't use Anglicism]."[36] Because this connotation of poch@ persists outside the U.S., the sentiment resonates tangentially. Moreover, the perpetuation of this kind of rhetoric exhibits how standards for identity continue to be dictated by colonial narratives. That these narratives crossover as a part of the tradition of migration in the Americas shows

DOI: 10.1057/9781137498076.0006

that the tensions "between cultural assimilation and otherness" remain a topos for pop culture.[37]

Bidi bidi pocha

Even though poch@ identity is closely tied to language, Américo Paredes posits that the negotiation of identity is a universal desire, one that I would argue is a strong appeal of poch@ pop: "the pocho's search for identity was a state shared by all Mexicans, and perhaps by all the world."[38] In *Selena* (1997), Jennifer Lopez stars as a crossover pop star negotiating a bi-cultural identity in a prominent biographical film about a poch@ musician in the U.S. A Tejana from Corpus Christi, Selena Quintanilla-Pérez grew up speaking English despite the fact that she would become famous for the songs she sang in Spanish. Following a similar narrative arch as *La Bamba*, the film details the interconnected familial and professional life of Selena, her musical successes, her romantic relationship with a guitar player in her accompanying band, concluding with the tragic death of the young musician.

Edward James Olmos persuasively portrays Selena's demanding father Abraham Quintanilla and appears overbearing in every facet of the young musician's life. In a scene where Olmos as Abraham is driving the family tour bus from one concert location to the next, Lopez and her character's brother sit up front listening to Olmos make what could be reductively interpreted as a humorous rant. Both Lopez and the actor portraying her brother gesture mockingly about their father's points of view, as though they were familiar with them but did not subscribe to them. Olmos as Abraham acknowledges the bi-cultural positionality of Mexican Americans in the U.S.-Mexico borderlands. Furthermore, he points out the rhetorical obligation to know and identify with both Anglo and Mexican audiences as well as their cultural references and worldviews:

> Being Mexican American is tough. Anglos jump all over you if you don't speak English perfectly. Mexicans jump all over you if you don't speak Spanish perfectly. We got to be twice as perfect as anybody else…I'm serious. Our family has been here for centuries and yet they treat us as if we just swam across the Rio Grande. I mean we got to know about John Wayne and Pedro Infante….We got to know about Oprah and Cristina…Ours [homeland] is right next door, right over there. And *we got to prove to the Mexicans how Mexican we are, and we got to prove to the Americans how American we are. We got to be more Mexican than the Mexicans and more American than the Americans,*

DOI: 10.1057/9781137498076.0006

both at the same time—it's exhausting. *Man*, nobody knows how tough it is to be Mexican American.[39]

The tension that Olmos' Abraham expresses highlights what Anzaldúa calls the *nepantla*, or the feeling of being torn between two cultures and two colonial standards.[40] Both the Anglo and Mexican colonial narratives hold Mexican Americans up to competing ideals and constructions of cultural authenticity that the colonized attempt to mimic, and ultimately fall short of.[41] In the genre of music, Olmos' monologue echoes a comparison that Valenzuela-Arce makes between the poch@ identity vis-à-vis a song by the artist Piporro: "*El Pocho incorpora la canción de Piporro: 'soy americano y mexicano y ninguno soy'* [The poch@ embodies the song by Piporro: I am American and Mexican and neither]."[42] Valenzuela-Arce applies the lyrics performed by a comedic actor-musician who was well-known for his portrayal of "norteño-types" to the analysis of poch@s because norteño-types along the border are considered to be neither pure Mexican nor American.

Olmos' monologue on the perceptions of Latin@s in the U.S. by Latin@ south of the U.S.-Mexico border describes the phenomenon for which poch@ was used to delineate. In *El Bandolero, el Pocho y la Raza*, David R. Maciel defines the use of poch@ "*para nombrar a los 'otros mexicanos', a los que vivían más allá del Río Bravo* [for naming those 'other Mexicans', those that live all the way out near the Rio Bravo]."[43] This description of poch@ identity as those living near the Rio Bravo, referred to as the Rio Grande in the U.S., indicates the added nuance of geographic location that complicates the narrow linguistic or cultural traitor characterizations. Maciel's description of poch@, however, fails to account for the "jump[ing] all over you if you don't speak Spanish perfectly" sentiment that Olmos's character in *Selena* criticizes.

The influence of the U.S. on culture in Mexico has a historical tradition that seemingly substantiates Olmos' monologue in *Selena*. Américo Paredes responds to Octavio Paz's claim that poch@s have lost their culture by citing newspapers and radio media as indicators of the shifting paradigm of cultural influence. Paredes writes:

> Reading Mexican periodicals and listening to Mexican radio and television, one gets the impression that in a cultural sense the border has shifted south a bit, to the point somewhere below Mexico City, let us say. And that may be why the younger Mexican intellectuals are more sympathetic toward the *pocho-chicano* than their elders were; they are much more aware of our problems. Because in this, Octavio Paz did not miss the mark. He was wrong

DOI: 10.1057/9781137498076.0006

in assuming that the Mexican American has lost all his heritage. But he was right in noting that the *pocho*, living between two cultures, existed in a state of permanent crisis; and that the *pocho's* search for identity was a state shared by all Mexicans, and perhaps by all the world.[44]

It is noteworthy that Parades' assertion about the impact of U.S. culture on Mexican culture can be evidenced through pop culture media. Poch@s remain responsible for the cultural-savvy that Olmos' example of needing to know both John Wayne and Pedro Infante demonstrates. Populations on both sides of the border employ these pop culture references, using them in the Burkean sense as cultural symbols which make sense of the world.[45] While pop culture can be dismissed as non-canonical, these productions in the U.S.-Mexico borderlands serve as cultural signposts that authorize and validate those consumers who recognize and follow them.

Parades' use of newspapers and radio as examples of the culture that crosses the border connects with the tangible effects of the real-life pop artist Selena. According to America Rodriguez, the inception of *People En Español* came about:

> [I]n response to the success of the *People* 1995 special edition on the murder of Selena, a Mexican American singer, which sold 400,000 copies. Several weeks later *People* published (also in English) a special commemorative Selena issue which sold one million copies at $3.95 each.[46]

As an icon, Selena's death caused tangible reverberations on the production of a pop culture medium that was entirely different from the musical medium in which she worked. Again, this kind of reception of Latin@ audiences in the U.S. displays the demand for pop culture reflecting bi-cultural experiences.

A note on current poch@ pop films

I conclude my proto-poch@ pop examination of films by traveling through time and space from *Selena* to nearly 20 years later and a film by Robert Rodriguez, who is no doubt the most successful poch@ pop producer[47]. In Rodriguez's *Machete* (2010), Danny Trejo stars in the title role as a former Mexican *federale* who is framed in an assassination plot against a Texas State Senator whose politics parallel the political discourse and policy passed in Arizona. Ultimately, Machete has his

DOI: 10.1057/9781137498076.0006

revenge and "gets the girl," portrayed by Jessica Alba, along the way. The subtext-free dialogue serves as a platform for the critique of political hot button issues such as immigration and border security under the guise of tongue-in-cheek B-movie action dialogue.

Employing strategic essentialism, Rodriguez as writer and director deploys offensive stereotypes in his straight-forward dialogue that satiate the expectations of uncritical audiences. Rodriguez appropriates the dehumanizing language of "illegal," "wetback," and "frito bandito" to reflect and critique real world social issues such as the presence of racism in Arizona's legislative border policy, passed during the production of the film. He understands the necessary rhetorical gestures to appeal to a mainstream audience with poch@ pop: "So I want to fool the audience into seeing the movie, and have them enjoy it, and not even have them realize that this is also about a Latino… I started to do that with *Desperado*."[48]

Jessica Alba's role as policewoman, Officer Sartana, provides an entry point into critical consciousness about the social inequality supported by racist legislation. In the third act, Alba's character Sartana spells out the social message: "Well there's the law and there's what's right…I am a woman of the law, and there are lots of laws. But if they don't offer us justice, then they aren't laws. They are just lines drawn in the sand by men who will stand on your backs for power and glory."[49] Not much later in the film, Alba echoes appropriated rhetorical phrasing from Malcolm X's famous "we didn't land on Plymouth rock, Plymouth rock landed on us" that came into the public consciousness with Denzel Washington's portrayal in Spike Lee's joint *Malcolm X* (1992). Alba stands on a car and yells, "We didn't cross the border, the border crossed us."[50] Alba's dialogue communicates necessary exposition for audiences to follow her critical recognition of racist policy that she by default enforces as a policewoman. The echoing of Malcolm X's famous rhetorical refrain on citizenship demonstrates parallels in "minority" rhetorics that respond to dominant white discourse about people of color. Indicative of public perception, Alba received the 2010 Razzie award for Worst Actress for her work in *Machete*, highlighting the difficulty of communicating a critical message in a genre film and the willingness of mainstream audiences to dismiss such critiques.

In an interview, Rodriguez acknowledges his effort in trying to bring more brown faces and stories into the cinematic spotlight.[51] In the context of having been honored with the Anthony Quinn Alma award,

DOI: 10.1057/9781137498076.0006

Rodriguez explained, "That's been my whole career. The past twenty years since *El Mariachi* seeing that there was a need for that, to change the face of Hollywood, what they were presenting, it was a struggle at first."[52] Rodriguez's enduring struggle can be seen as a continuation of the work begun by *Zoot Suit* and *La Bamba* writer and director Luis Valdez. Before Rodriguez, Valdez confronted the same issue of "[w]orking within the dominant cinematic industry...[and] how political artists negotiate social commitment with the exigencies of appealing to mainstream audiences."[53] Valdez's work demonstrates a skillful performance of subversive complicity because he was able to navigate the dominant cinematic industry on multiple occasions, achieving success that has crossed over into the collective cultural memory of this generation of poch@ pop audiences. Although the films *La Bamba* and *Selena* differ greatly from films such as *Machete* and *From Dusk Till Dawn*, the shift of poch@ stories from the margins to center stage remains a strategic decision that is rhetorically negotiated.

Conclusion

The identification of proto-poch@ pop provides more than just a foundation upon which more contemporary cultural producers build and oppose dominant cultural narratives of deficiency. By calling attention to films such as *Stand and Deliver*, *Selena*, and *La Bamba*, I also indict films like *187*, *The Substitute*, and *Dangerous Minds* that misrepresent Latin@ culture and normalize cliché representations of fiery Latinas and banditos. Unfortunately, proto-poch@ pop films arose as relative anomalies within a media system that commits acts of erasure in the representation of the socially constructed "Other." Robert Rodriguez's admission that socially conscious rhetoric in films continues to be subversive serves as a reminder that resistance to internalized colonialism and neocolonial narratives requires that the message be encoded in a satirical or irreverent genre. Genres such as films, political cartoons, political satire and performance art provide interstitial spaces in the pop culture landscape where poch@ pop artists create productions that contest, challenge, and interrupt politicized discourse.

In the U.S., pop culture marks life events and instantiates widely-held interpretations of the historical moments affixed through the taxonomies configured by cultural productions specific to that time and space.

DOI: 10.1057/9781137498076.0006

Whether good or bad, pop culture provides role models for students, teachers, artists, and mainstream audiences. Edward James Olmos continues to influence pop culture with his Olmos production company, spanning his early career with *The Ballad of Gregorio Cortez* (1982) to *Americanos: Latino Life in the United States* (2002), clear through to recent films such as *Filly Brown* (2012) and *El Americano: The Movie* (2014). Meanwhile, Robert Rodriguez continues to be one of the most successful poch@ pop producers with his Spanish language film *El Mariachi* (1992), and his subsequent ability to generate crossover appeal for culturally-relevant films such as *Desperado* (1994), *Once Upon a Time in Mexico* (2003), *Machete* (2010), *Machete Kills* (2013) in addition to collaborations with writer-director Quentin Tarantino like *Four Rooms* (1995), *From Dusk till Dawn* (1996), *Sin City* (2005), and *Grindhouse: Death Proof and Planet Terror* (2007). Rodriguez's film career is a testament to his understanding of how to navigate the mainstream system of media while doing his best to work against the system's tendency towards cultural erasure.

In Chapter 3, I more fully enunciate the theories and methods that inform and embody poch@ as a decolonial trope and poch@ pop as a contemporary brand of culture created to entertain and subvert neoliberal and ultraconservative narratives. The ambiguity of poch@ and its pejorative connotations contribute to the rhetorical efficacy of its current (re)appropriation, while rooting itself in a longer tradition of migration in the U.S. and the negotiation of bi-cultural experiences.

Notes

1   Jencks and Phillips 1998.
2   Fregoso 1993; Tatum 2001.)
3   Garcia 2013.
4   See Medina 2013a; 2013b; 2014a; 2014b.
5   Douglas qtd. in Rodriguez 1997, 293.
6   Fregoso 1993; Tatum 2001.
7   Keller 1994, 207 qtd. in Tatum 2001, 59.
8   Fregoso 1993; Pérez 1999; Tatum 2001.
9   Báez 2007; Beltran 2002; Guzman and Valdivia 2004.
10   Anzaldúa 1987.
11   Holling 2008, 297.
12   Tatum 2001.
13   Yosso 2002.

DOI: 10.1057/9781137498076.0006

14   Keller 1994 qtd. in Tatum 2001, 61.
15   Barthes 1972, 15.
16   Calvo 2002, 73.
17   Ramírez-Berg 2002, 250–251.
18   Anzaldúa 1987, 68.
19   Anzaldúa 1987, 68.
20   Fregoso 1993, 21.
21   Fregoso 1993, 22.
22   Holling 2008, 300.
23   Ramírez-Berg 2002, 254.
24   Nericcio 2007, 85–86.
25   Rodriguez 1983, 1.
26   Beltran 2002, 82.
27   Guzmán and Valdivia 2004, 207.
28   Guzmán 2006, 246.
29   Báez 2007.
30   *La Bamba* 1987.
31   Anzaldúa 1987; Rodriguez 1982; Villarreal 1959.
32   Rosales 1997.
33   Holling 2008, 298.
34   Fregoso 1993, 40.
35   Valenzuela-Arce 2004, 130.
36   Valenzuela-Arce 2004, 132.
37   Avila-Saavedra 2011.
38   Paredes 1993, 47.
39   *Selena* 1997.
40   Anzaldúa 1987, 78.
41   Bhabha 1994.
42   Author's translation, Valenzuela-Arce 2004, 132.
43   Maciel 2000, 84.
44   Paredes 1993, 47.
45   Burke 1966.
46   Rodriguez 1999, 301
47   Although I identify Edward James Olmos as iconic, Robert Rodriguez's channel the El Rey Network stands as testament to his success.
48   Ramírez-Berg 2002, 246.
49   Rodriguez and Maniquis 2002.
50   Rodriguez and Maniquis 2002.
51   Rodriguez again explains this intention during his Corazon de Oro acceptance speech.
52   Garcia 2013.
53   Fregoso 1993, 23.

DOI: 10.1057/9781137498076.0006

3

Poch@ Methodological (Re)appropriation for Resistance: Poch@ Past

Abstract: *Chapter 3 outlines the theoretical and methodological framework that explains the resistance to colonial narratives that subjugate Latin@s in the U.S. Poch@ artists (re)appropriate rhetoric and symbols that frame Latin@s as culturally deficient according to colonial standards. Emma Pérez's theory of the decolonial imaginary provides a framework for how artist reveal the possibilities for resistance outside of dominant colonial narratives. In addition, the* rascuache *methodology that Guillermo Gómez-Peña identifies reveals how the use of the pejorative term "pocho" serves as an appropriation that challenges deficiency-based colonial narratives. Gómez-Peña resists deficit rhetoric by re-claiming the trope of poch@ and by challenging the outdated colonial binary paradigm, evidenced by the naming of his troupe La Pocha Nostra and a character Pocho-Dos.*

Medina, Cruz. *Reclaiming Poch@ Pop: Examining the Rhetoric of Cultural Deficiency.* New York: Palgrave Macmillan, 2015. DOI: 10.1057/9781137498076.0007.

DOI: 10.1057/9781137498076.0007

In an interview with Telemundo's online channel *Mun2*, pop culture icon Edward James Olmos revealed his perspective and experience with the trope of poch@. Olmos' description centers around the pejorative connotation of poch@ that his generation of U.S.-born Latin@s experienced, and the residual negative feelings associated with the trope. Olmos explains:

> Pocho has always been a person of Mexican descent, but born outside of the country [of Mexico]. At one point in the 50s and 60s, it was a really difficult word to carry because it was really used derogatorily. It was a common used word when it came to Mexicans that were born in the United States and maybe didn't speak Spanish correctly... Pocho is again, that's a word that was given, that's used by people say in Mexico towards people who are from the United States of Mexican descent.[1]

Although Olmos attributes the origins of poch@ to the people of Mexico, the broader-reaching role of colonialism and neocolonialism should not be dismissed. After all, measuring the correctness of Spanish, as Olmos describes, functions as a colonial apparatus for dividing a colonized population; constructed measures of "correctly" speaking the colonial language reinforce either/or colonial binaries that ultimately position the colonized subject as deficient.[2] For Olmos, poch@ signified the shame for speaking Spanish "incorrectly" and its tenuous function as indicator of rejecting Mexican heritage and culture. In *Borderlands/La Frontera*, Gloria Anzaldúa depicts a scene similar to what Olmos experienced with regard to poch@. In her widely anthologized piece "How to Tame a Wild Tongue," Anzaldúa describes how the pejorative connotation of poch@ is deeply rooted in its influence on language:

> "*Pocho*, cultural traitor, you're speaking the oppressor's language by speaking English, you're ruining the Spanish language," I have been accused by various Latinos and Latinas... Words distorted by English are known as anglicisms or *pochismos*. The *pocho* is an anglicized Mexican or American of Mexican origin who speaks Spanish with an accent characteristic of North Americans and who distorts and reconstructs the language according to the influence of English.[3]

In the same section, Anzaldúa acknowledges the presence of those within Latin@ communities who internalize and perform colonial gate-keeping. Illuminating education's role as a hegemonic apparatus, Anzaldúa argues that Spanish speakers exert control by *reglas*, or colonial rules: "other Spanish speakers *nos quieren poner candados en la boca*. They would hold us back with their bag of *reglas de academia*."[4] Deficiency rhetoric undergirds the colonial and neocolonial narratives about Mexican Americans

DOI: 10.1057/9781137498076.0007

that position them in opposition to one another, which undermines internal community-building and resistance to external subjugation.

Examining television comedy, communication researcher Guillermo Avila-Saavedra interprets tensions over language in the U.S. He concludes with the unfortunate perception that many Latin American migrant families possess raising children in the U.S.: "The linguistic dilemma means that, although U.S. bilingual Latinos 'should' embrace a notion of ethnic pride symbolized in Spanish fluency, they may actually covet the social power that is embedded in the use of English."[5] An important rhetorical element of poch@ pop producers is their ability to negotiate and appropriate translingual language and grammar without resigning to the neocolonial ideologies reinstituted by Standard English and English-only policies in the U.S.

Because of the colonial paradigm that imposes ideological boundaries between Mexican and Mexican American communities, it is understandable why the consciousness of the Chicano civil rights movement similarly opposed assimilation and Anglo culture.[6] At the same time, depictions of poch@ as a cultural traitor endured because of texts such as Richard Rodriguez's *Hunger of Memory*, which supports assimilation while opposing bilingual education. Since the rhetorical efficacy of *Hunger of Memory* was its ethos as an "authentic minority" perspective, Victor Villanueva problematizes Rodriguez's minority icon status by pointing out the "ideological resignation" that undermines his credibility. Villanueva cogently argues that "Rodriguez's success comes to great degree from his arguing the case for assimilation even as his own assimilation is denied him."[7] Rodriguez's experience as a poch@ provides insight into the neocolonial narratives and deficiency rhetoric that poch@ pop producers disrupt. It is, however, worth noting how his political alignment regarding language and culture contribute to colonial narratives becoming normalized in public discourse. In a demonstration of progress, producers of poch@ pop culture appeal to a bicultural experience while honoring heritage culture.

This chapter illuminates the colonial paradigm that undergirds and provides the agenda for cultural deficiency rhetoric that permeates mainstream pop culture and politics, reifying these beliefs into laws and policy that subjugate Latin@s in the U.S. Beyond the colonial narratives transmitted through history, this chapter examines the *rascuache* methodology that performance artist Guillermo Gómez-Peña articulates, and which other poch@ pop producers employ. Poch@ pop producers

DOI: 10.1057/9781137498076.0007

extend and complicate the message of Villanueva's *Bootstraps* by countering the myth that frames students of color as deficient if they are unable
to "pull themselves up." The bootstraps rhetoric, which Villanueva
demystifies, works against cross-cultural collaboration. More recently,
Aja Y. Martinez exposes the rhetoric of the American Dream as a myth
that facilitates "colorblind" racism, similarly serving to push minoritized
voices to the margins.[8] Fortunately, the agency and ethos of a *rascuache*
methodology that poch@ artists utilize makes due with what is at hand
even if there is no community network or platform for support. Poch@
pop producers repurpose hegemonic mainstream symbols and genres,
often engaging with issues and cultural deficiency rhetoric covered by
mainstream and conservative media.

The reclamation of poch@ by Lalo Alcaraz for his news and satire
website *Pocho.com* and for his *Pocho Hour of Power* radio show were
perhaps some of the earliest re-purposing of the pejorative trope,
which I discuss in Chapter 4. Still others have similarly embraced
the poch@ moniker. A short list should include performance artist
Guillermo Gómez-Peña naming his troupe La Pocha Nostra, jour-
nalist Daniel Hernandez identifies as poch@ in the motherland in
his non-fiction account *Down and Delirious in Mexico City: The Aztec
Metropolis in the 21st Century*,[9] academic and South El Monte Art Posse
(SEMAP) co-director Romeo Guzman named his blog *Pocho in Greater
Mexico*, and photographer Pocho1 documents many cultural events
that celebrate the *mestizaje* of Pre-Columbian tradition and Chican@
community activism. In Chapter 4, I also discuss how the *Daily Show's*
Al Madrigal draws attention to the continued lack of representation in
the media as an entry point to examining the work of *Pocho.com's* Lalo
Alcaraz. First, I would here to provide historical context that outlines
some rhetorical disruptions of colonial narratives promoting cultural
deficiency.

A history of (mis)representation

Unfortunately, the number of people with Latin American heritage
in English-language media industries remains low,[10] a phenomenon
dismissed by both mainstream neoliberal and ultraconservative news
outlets and politicians alike.[11] For me, the long summer days spent on
my grandmother's itchy couch watching *I Love Lucy* (1951–1957) re-runs

DOI: 10.1057/9781137498076.0007

showed me that Spanish-speakers could make it onto TV. Back then, I thought little of Desi Arnez's place as a Cuban-born performer on TV, or as Guillermo Avila-Saavedra points out: "Ricky Ricardo was an economically successful, socially assimilated Latino. He provided a reasonably positive Latino image that was a constant presence in U.S. homes for more than 6 years."[12] Avila-Saavedra hits the proverbial nail on the head with his description of Ricardo as "assimilated" because of his presentable representation, with only bursts of Spanish that were meant to "spice-up" his dialogue as ethnic "Other" for comedic purposes. For Cuban American actor Arnez, his experience differed from those of many Mexican American actors:

> From the earliest days, the vast majority of roles for Mexican American actors in Hollywood formula films were the Castilian *caballero* (romantic male), dark lady, greaser-gangster, social problem, Good Samaritan, and brown avenger. Typically, the Mexican Americans who played these roles were killed, mocked, punished, seduced, or saved from poverty, moral ruin, or death by Anglo actors playing socially redeeming roles.[13]

While it could be argued that Lucille Ball served as Arnez's redeemer, Arnez crossed cultural boundaries performing Caribbean music while married to an Anglo comedic icon. Knowing my own parents' struggle to have their marriage accepted by my Anglo mother's parents, I recognize the progressive accomplishment by Arnez and Ball during this time period.[14]

During the same era, the life and career of actress Rita Hayworth reveals how the movie industry erases the culture of on a Mexican American, as discussed by Edén Torres and William Nericcio.[15] Pointing out changes to her name, hair and skin color, Nericcio argues that the exotification of Mexican Americans in the U.S.—with heightened sexuality and violence projected onto them—compels them to whitewash the identities they perform. In addition, Nericcio traces the symbolism of Speedy Gonzalez, arriving at the conclusion that the cartoon mouse is a simulacrum for racial stereotypes. Similarly in rhetoric and composition, Octavio Pimentel and Paul Velázquez critically examine the portrayal of people of color in *Shrek 2* (2004) by looking at the film's use of stereotypical language.[16] Pimentel and Velázquez draw comparisons between the animated film and the reproduction of racist ideologies that reinforce social inequality in the U.S. Like Nericcio's work, Pimentel and Velázquez engage in analysis of pop cultural productions in order to illuminate the

DOI: 10.1057/9781137498076.0007

existence and perpetuation of racist assumptions embedded in stereotypical media representations.

Pop culture such as *Shrek 2* and *I Love Lucy* draw much of their rhetorical efficacy via humor, although the assumptions embedded in the representations of ethnic "Others" remain problematic. Unlike pop culture that represents people of color as ethnic "Others," the rhetorical productions by poch@s disrupt this tradition of misrepresentation by addressing issues affecting these communities. Avila-Saavedra explains that one of the topoi that Latin@ comedians derive tension from is the assimilation for which Ricky Ricardo was celebrated:

> Comedy is an interesting site to investigate the symbolic articulation of ethnic identities and the power of media representation to challenge or reinforce ethnic stereotypes...Latino television comedians articulate an implicit tension between ethnic otherness and desire for assimilation for U.S. Latinos.[17]

Strangely, even when some Latin@ producers create their own pop culture, the rhetoric of cultural deficiency lies beneath the misrepresentations from without and the tensions from within the Latin@ community. As a rhetorical element, humor transgresses the privilege afforded to logos by the Greco-Roman tradition, wherein logic could be trusted, while humor as an appeal to pathos was not. In *Chicano Satire: A Study in Literary Culture*, Guillermo Hernández explains that poch@ has an established tradition as a trope in the genre of comedy,[18] which helps to explain the ambiguity of the trope and why comedy is a salient rhetorical strategy of poch@ pop producers.

Tropes, deficiency rhetoric, and decolonial imaginary

In *A Grammar of Motives*, Kenneth Burke recognizes the persuasive power of what he called the "master tropes": metaphor, metonymy, synecdoche, and irony. The notion of the master tropes—which Burke simply describes as the "thisness of a that, or the thatness of a this"[19]—inspired African American literary scholar Henry Louis Gates to appropriate the figurative power of the "master tropes" in order to subvert it. Gates does so by naming an African American literary and political trope that reclaims a once pejorative trope. In *The Signifying Monkey: A Theory of Afro-American Literary Criticism*, Gates explains how a trope for African-American literary theory responds to this tradition:

DOI: 10.1057/9781137498076.0007

If Vico and Burke, or Nietzsche, de Man, and Bloom, are correct in identifying four and six "master tropes," then we might think of these as the "master's
tropes," and of Signifyin(g) as the slave's trope, the trope of tropes, as Bloom
characterizes metalepsis, "a trope-reversing trope, a figure of a figure."[20]

While Gates identifies what he calls the "slave's trope" through a process
of symbol switching, the meaning of the tropes are not lost or forgotten.
Instead, their meanings resist and respond to previous misinterpreta-
tions. Much like Gates' (re)appropriation of the "slave" trope signifyin(g),
I posit that poch@ functions as a rhetorical trope that subsumes and
appropriates authorized and documented rhetoric for resistant poch@
pop producers in the U.S.

Because of the rhetorical power of poch@, the appropriation of the
trope by pop culture producers in the U.S. speaks to their recognition of
what the trope has the possibility to signify. For performance artist and
cultural critic Guillermo Gómez-Peña, the trope of "pocho" is one that
he regards as an outdated pejorative for cultural traitor, yet he continues
to draw on the rhetorical efficacy by naming his theater company La
Pocha Nostra. Criticizing the pre-Zapatista era in Mexico, Gómez-Peña
describes poch@ as having a narrow definition of identity based on colonial values regarding language:

> In those days, the notion of identity was closely linked to language and terri-
> tory. If you spoke Spanish and lived in Mexico, you were Mexican. And if
> you crossed the border you *ipso-facto* became a renegade, a traitor, a pocho.
> That was a complete fallacy based on a very old-fashioned binary model of
> identity.[21]

Clearly, Gómez-Peña resists colonial narratives and plays on the cultural
ambiguity of the trope. His motivation for reclaiming poch@ additionally challenges the colonial paradigm, or imaginary, that Emma Pérez
identifies in the construction of historical records, which become
normalized through the cultural production of writing.[22] Furthermore,
Pérez explains that "traditionalist historiography produces a fictive
past, and that fiction becomes the knowledge manipulated to negate the
'other' culture's differences."[23] These fictional historical narratives dismiss
the agency of the colonized and subaltern as an apparatus of colonialism, while reinforcing the constructed ethnic identities such as poch@ as
lacking culture and language.

True to form, many stereotypes about people of color in the U.S. mirror
the exotification of the "Other" that colonial forces attribute to subaltern

populations, thereby mischaracterizing them as childlike, overly sexual, and violent. In *Jennifer as Selena: Rethinking Latinidad in Media and Popular Culture*, Frances R. Aparicio examines the construction of Tejana identity, Latina subjectivities, and the struggle with "hegemonic notions of physical beauty" in order to address the enduring colonial role of mainstream media.[24] Drawing on Pérez's decolonial framework, Aparicio points out that language maintains a colonial role in mainstream media programming:

> a Latina experience constituted by a history of cultural, linguistic, and economic colonization that both Selena and Jennifer López have embodied, particularly in terms of their dominant language as English-speaking Latinas...the inverse colonization, one may say, of Spanish-cable television programming, suggests that US Latino/as as audiences still do not have media productions that are controlled nationally or mostly produced by our own communities.[25]

Language plays a pivotal role in the performance of Latin@ identity, or latinidad: even the early definition of poch@ as cultural traitor was often linked to the inability to speak Spanish. Following colonial logic, Aparicio identifies English with colonial power while aligning the Spanish language with the colonized, despite the fact that both English and Spanish were the languages of power over the indigenous of the Americas. Similar to the Latina feminism that Aparicio attributes to *Selena*, poch@ pop artists create cultural productions in English that challenge the enduring colonial fictions in ultraconservative legislative policy.

To summarize, the 1980s representation of people of Latin American heritage in mainstream popular culture was nearly non-existent, except for clichéd representations with embedded racist assumptions framing them as outlaws, lazy, childlike, or highly sexualized. While the film *Zoot Suit* (1981) marks a moment when Luis Valdez wrote and directed a film with a predominantly Latin@ cast, the success of the film could be attributed to the familiar outlaw subject matter that mainstream Anglo audiences have been acculturated to expect. By the late eighties, Valdez achieved greater mainstream success with *La Bamba* (1987), a film that broke from the well-trodden stereotypical subject matter, instead, presenting the true story of American-born rock and roll musician Ritchie Valens' biography. As posited in the previous chapter, *La Bamba* provides a salient example of proto-poch@ pop because of the central focus on a U.S. Latino who successfully produces popular culture, while

DOI: 10.1057/9781137498076.0007

navigating the erasure of mainstream U.S. culture by appropriating traditional Mexican folk music.

Similarly, the biopic of U.S.-born Tejana Selena Quintanilla-Pérez, *Selena* (1997), has provided an influential representation of an artist navigating the border culture of the Tejana music industry while additionally producing symbolic resistance to colonial constructions of Latin@ identity. The film *Selena* as well as Salma Hayek's portrayal of the title role in *Frida* (2002) create generative examples of cinematic pop culture that complicate the issues of representation and racist ideologies by drawing on issues of gender, transnational identity, feminist symbolism, and aesthetics of ethnic bodies and the impact on mainstream audiences. The possibility for these rhetorical productions to complicate existing cultural narratives is yet another reason to examine the pop culture productions of poch@s in the U.S.: the genre of film provides salient examples of poch@s negotiating and challenging the expectations of mainstream audiences. However, contemporary poch@ pop extends the work of positive representations such as Valens and Selena through outspoken artistic work; this works succeeds in resisting cultural deficiency rhetoric that persists in politics, news, policy, and exclusionary mainstream pop culture.

Hemispheric shifts and mestiz@ rhetorics

The issues raised by the films *Frida* and *Selena*, including language, Latinidad, feminism, and sexual objectification parallel the themes raised in the cultural productions of poch@ pop producers. The critical responses to *Selena* are in line with René Agustín De los Santos' discussion of the recent trends in Latin@ rhetorical scholarship that recognizes the broadening of issues related to representation and beyond. In particular, De los Santos notes the important re-imagining of "rhetorical studies in the United States as part of a larger hemispheric history of communicative practices and interactions"; this book follows the trend De los Santos identifies by further complicating representations of resistance and negotiation while drawing on the "larger American hemispheric endeavor, [that] will require a subtle but important shift" in how rhetorical scholarship extends existing scholarship and creates new spaces for inquiry.[26] Perhaps one of the most salient examples of the larger hemispheric endeavor that De los Santos refers to includes

DOI: 10.1057/9781137498076.0007

Damian Baca's *Mestiz@ Scripts, Digital Migrations and the Territories of Writing*. Much like the discussion of poch@ as a reclaimed trope of resistance, Baca discusses the trope of "mestiz@," which describes the people in the Americas with mixed Indigenous and European heritage, and the contested legitimacy of racial identity that de-authorizes indigenous knowledge, histories, and literacy practices.[27] Just as poch@ is challenged by some members of the Latin@ community as to whether it is an authentic performance of latinidad, Baca notes that, "Mestiz@s have continually faced dichotomous narratives that call the legitimacy of their existence into question."[28] When considering the issues that poch@ pop producers address, Baca's explanation of mestiz@ experience prophetically parallels the situation of Latin@s in Arizona after the passing of Senate Bill 1070.[29] The legislation that allowed for local law enforcement to question any "reasonably suspicious" person about their legal status signals yet another point in the continuum of calling the legitimacy of brown bodies into question.

Although poch@ pop can resist dehumanizing legislation such as SB 1070, which impacts and separates families, the strategy of humor rhetorically juxtaposes with the serious nature of these issues, thereby increasing the efficacy of their subversive messages. As in genres of news satire and political cartoons, the irreverence of poch@ pop producers facilitates appeals to Latin@ and non-Latin@ audiences. The rhetorical power of poch@ as a trope comes in part from what Jennifer Alvarez Dickinson describes as "a 'pocho aesthetic' that is rebellious and playful, yet frequently reveals anxieties over citizenship and representations in American culture."[30] The poch@ aesthetic is very much situated in the rhetorical appeal to pathos and provides the pop culture productions with a complicit primary commercial message. In the genre of comedy, *Ugly Betty* (2006–2010)—from the Spanish language *Yo soy Betty, la fea* (1999–2001)—provides a generative intersection of representation and the politics of legal status. Hector Amaya explains that *Ugly Betty*:

> relies on the systematic marginalization of Latino labor in the industry and in legal frameworks of citizenship, as well as on a definition of diversity tuned more to corporate interests than to social justice. After decades of legal and activist efforts, it remains difficult for Latinas/os to participate in mainstream English-language media. This is the result of a complex of cultural practices and law…that produce differentiated citizenship experiences.[31]

Amaya's focus on citizenship and the law as an interpretive framework illuminates how pop culture narratives reinforce mainstream

DOI: 10.1057/9781137498076.0007

assumptions about citizenship. Still, Amaya's overall thesis that media normalizes notions of diversity without improving social standings is a familiar return to earlier, non-legal criticism. However, Amaya's attention to legal framework relegates the subject matter of the comedic genre as devoid of humor in contrast with the playful rebelliousness of a poch@ aesthetic. Even though Amaya expresses a valid argument about the normalizing effect of pop culture on important issues like immigration policy, Amaya ignores the rhetorical element of humor and the ability of pop culture to appeal to audiences with pathos while communicating messages embedded with logos.

Poch@ pop artist-producers

During the historical moment in 2010 when Arizona passed both SB 1070 and HB 2281, some of the most resistant, irreverent, and controversial voices producing media and art had branded themselves with the label poch@. Political cartoonist Lalo Alcaraz has embraced the trope as co-editor of the *Pocho.com*'s website, host of the *Pocho Hour of Power* radio show, and collaborator with Pocho Productions and National Pochismo Institute, unabashedly transgressing the once pejorative connotation of "cultural traitor."[32] Alcaraz's social satire poignantly critiques important issues affecting poch@s such as immigration, exploitation, racism, bilingualism, and education. At the same time, Alcaraz complicates the representation of brown folk,[33] playing with and against stereotypes and deficiency rhetoric.

In May of 2013, when Disney attempted to copyright the Latin American holiday Dia de los Muertos for a movie and the merchandise related to the film, Lalo Alcaraz responded with the image "Muerto Mouse" that disseminated throughout social media. The visual rhetoric of "Muerto Mouse" contested the globalizing effects of the transnational media industrial complex that subsumes and erases cultural difference, having transmitted rhizomatically through social networks.[34] As a tangible result of Alcaraz's rhetorically crafted message, Disney withdrew their application for copyright.[35] Like much of Alcaraz's poch@ pop, his critique of Disney employed the "pocho humor" that Dickinson explains as "rebel[ling] against a range of norms... [and] the humor of those who feel caught between cultures can be defensive, work to construct new norms, and reinforce old prejudices."[36] The prejudices practiced by the

DOI: 10.1057/9781137498076.0007

FIGURE 3.1   *Muerto Mouse*

DOI: 10.1057/9781137498076.0007

media and represented in the media perform a dialectical relationship with the poch@ producers who may play the essentialism game strategically, if only to subvert the exposed assumptions.

Performance artist Guillermo Gómez-Peña similarly provides an important demonstration of a self-identifying poch@ pop producer. Gómez-Peña named his theater troupe, La Pocha Nostra, reclaiming poch@ in much the same ways as Alcaraz. In an interview with *Art Practical*, Gómez-Peña describes his reasoning for the use of poch@:

> It's essentially a neologism. "Pocho/a" means a cultural traitor, or a cultural bastard. It's a term coined by Mexicans who never left Mexico to articulate the post-national Mexican experience. It's slightly derogative, but we have expropriated it as an act of empowerment. And "Nostra" comes from La Cosa Nostra, the Italian mafia. So you can translate it loosely as the cartel of the cultural traitors, or there is another more poetic translation that essentially means "our impurities."[37]

Gómez-Peña's appropriation, which he refers to as "expropriation," of poch@ for empowerment demonstrates the tongue-in-cheek subversiveness that characterizes the poch@ aesthetic and humor. In addition, Gómez-Peña has incorporated characters such as Pocho-Dos into his performances to further tease out the bi-cultural symbolism. Because Gómez-Peña's genre of performance art communicates messages with political import, the choice of naming his troupe and character poch@ extends beyond the level of superficial entertainment.

Even when subversive appropriation is a part of an artist's methodology, historical context should be considered, so as to acknowledge the work of predecessors. Responding to Gómez-Peña's *Dangerous Border Crossers*, Frederick Luis Aldama draws attention to Gómez-Peña's failure to contextualize his work within a larger network:

> Unfortunately, *Dangerous Border Crossers* fails to situate Gómez-Peña and Pocha Nostra's performances within a long tradition of Latino/a performance art that includes the work of Culture Clash, Carmelita Tropicana, Vaginal Davis, and Marga Gomez, to name a few; thus Gómez-Peña's artistry is set up as if sui generis, as if he is not a part of a larger network of artists who have been working to destabilize a racist and sexist American mainstream.[38]

Gómez-Peña's work seemingly falls into the category of artist who produces without citing sources, although his explicit incorporation of Pre-Columbian history such as the High-Tech Aztec character exhibits numerous historical inspirations.

DOI: 10.1057/9781137498076.0007

In Chapter 5, I discuss in more detail Gómez-Peña's collaboration with other artists in a pictographic re-imagining of a Mesoamerican codex. The *Codex Espangliensis* provides an especially important point of departure into the epistemology employed by poch@s who intersperse Pre-Columbian images with appropriations of iconic American pop culture imagery such as Superman and Mickey Mouse. The notion of "mestiz@ memory" that describes the Pre-Columbian cultural memory of Indigenous and European roots is helpful for accounting why Gómez-Peña might perform symbolic resistance without explicit documentation because it "symbolically opposes the triumph of conquest and assimilation."[39] What makes some of the productions of poch@ pop subversive is how these cultural texts resist proclaiming their opposition; rather, they appear to be complicit with mainstream assumptions, worldviews, and expectations.

Pre-Columbian poch@

As in the work of Damian Baca,[40] a historical perspective that incorporates Pre-Columbian cultural literacy practices symbolizes an explicit break from colonial narratives about poch@s in the U.S. The epistemology derived from Pre-Columbian rhetorical productions possesses particular import for the trope of poch@. One of the clearest connections between Mesoamerican history and poch@ takes place in the *Pocho Handbook*, a text which sought to bring together what the anonymous authors perceived as the fractured Mexican heritage communities of Chicanos, Mexican-Americans, and Pochos in the early eighties. Attributed to the collective Pocho Cultures Research and Development, the *Pocho Handbook* decolonizes poch@ through the etymological and historical connection with the pochteca, a Pre-Columbian traveling merchant described in book nine of the *Florentine Codex* by Bernadino de Sahagún. The anonymous writers of the *Handbook* assert that:

> [T]he Chicano who has become the Aztec is much like ancient times when the Chichimec became the Aztec. But as the Chicano becomes the new Aztec or the reborn Aztec, so the Pocho, as your namesake, becomes the new Pochteca or the reborn Pochteca.[41]

Because the *Pocho Handbook* has a collective author and provides no citations, academic claims against the validity and credibility of the material

DOI: 10.1057/9781137498076.0007

could be made in much the same way that non-white rhetorical traditions have been dismissed. Fortunately, Franciscan friar Bernadino de
Sahagún documents the pochteca, to which the *Pocho Handbook* draws
connections with the poch@ identity. In the sixteenth century *Florentine
Codex*, Sahagún provides details about that the merchants which reveal
rhetorical elements consistent with poch@ pop producers. Sahagún notes
that the pochteca were given the name of "disguised merchants": "in order
to disguise themselves, they took on the appearance of the [natives]. As
was the manner of cutting the hair of the people of Tzinacantlan…just
so did the merchants cut their hair to imitate them. And they learned
their tongue to enter in disguise."[42] Considering the name changes, the
coloring of hair, and speech accommodations of poch@ pop artists over
the course of their careers, the strategy that Sahagún identifies becomes
particularly apparent. In *The Aztecs*, Richard Townsend traces the etymological root of pochteca still deeper, and reveals a clearer connection
with the contemporary "pocho." Townsend explains, "The term pochotl,
from which pochteca and Pochtlán derive, was the same for the Bombax
ceiba, the towering, sheltering tree of the tropical forests."[43] I return to
this discussion of the pochteca and Pre-Columbian rhetorical practices
in Chapter 5, where I closely examine Guillermo Gómez-Peña's contemporary codex collaboration.

Rascuache methodology

Alcaraz's appropriation of the iconic Mickey Mouse imagery, in order to
criticize Disney's intention to commodify a cultural practice from across
Latin America, illuminates an important rhetorical strategy that serves as
a methodology for poch@ pop producers. The appropriation of imagery
by Disney parallels the very same (re)appropriation, reimagining or
expropriation of poch@ by artists such as Alcaraz and Gómez-Peña. The
theoretical underpinnings of this methodology stem from what has been
described as a *rascuache* sensibility. Guillermo Gómez-Peña describes
how *rascuache* serves as a methodology that employs available materials:
"[t]hese strategies of recycling and recontextualizing ideas, images and
texts continue to be central aspect of our performance methodology."[44]
Rascuache provides a generative way for not only recognizing the methodology that contributes to the aesthetic of poch@ pop culture, but also

DOI: 10.1057/9781137498076.0007

for understanding how the appropriation of dominant culture serves to subvert it. I posit that the production of poch@ pop embodies a *rascuache* (re)appropriation of cultural symbols, given how the trope of poch@ is recontexutalized outside of its connotation that is deeply embedded in colonial discourse about authenticity. Artists and producers who self-identify as poch@ do so with a decolonial ethos because the trope has yet to be subsumed by hegemonic U.S. discourse such as political discussions of voting populations.

Though my own methodology for examining poch@ pop texts is rhetorical and informed by cultural materialism, I also approach these texts from a historically-situated decolonial framework. Wendy Hesford describes cultural materialist methods as:

> [R]eading practices that foreground rhetoric [and] open up the space to consider how autobiographical subjects negotiate and claim a sense of agency among contrary discourses and how autobiographical subject and material body are cultural and linguistic sites of contestation.[45]

I interpret the "contrary discourses" that Hesford mentions as the colonial, neocolonial, and neoliberal narratives, which Pérez explains become normalized as a part of history or the "fictive past, and that fiction becomes the knowledge manipulated to negate the 'other' culture's differences."[46] Amid competing narratives and discourses of citizenship, legality, and authenticity, autobiography provides necessary disruptions. Pérez's decolonial theory, meanwhile, serves as a reminder of the colonial paradigm, from which these discourses derive power and authority. In rhetoric, Morris Young similarly highlights colonialism's impact on authorized forms of literacy: "*Literature of the contact zone* is the fiction authored in colonial contexts or out of colonial histories...forcing a sanctioned literacy on colonized subjects."[47] Previously, Victor Villanueva made the case for the application of decolonial theory when he explains that "[t]he demand for linguistic and rhetorical compliance still smacks of colonialism, practices which reproduce, in effect, the colonial histories of America's people of color."[48] Therefore, the decolonial evaluation of subversive texts provides a generative heuristic for cultural productions created by a *rascuache* methodology, given that both approaches strategically draw from hegemonic productions without ascribing to the accompanying ideology.

In Chapter 2, I identify *La Bamba* and *Selena* as proto-poch@ pop culture productions as a part of the work of artists crossing-over and appealing to mainstream audiences while performing culturally-relevant musical practices. During the production of *La Bamba*, Fregoso describes a filming schedule that sounds like a *rascuache* method of making due with resources at hand. Fregoso explains that "[f]orced to shoot the film in less than two weeks, Valdez explains much of the mise-en-scene's theatrical quality—in other words, the film's recourse to theater props for scenes—as the result of limited financial resources."[49] Although the work of poch@ pop artists appeals to mainstream audiences, David Spener frankly remarks that *rascuache* is associated with "los *de abajo*[the poorest class]," yet he focuses on the intrepid skills of "resourcefulness and ingenuity allowing the oppressed to overcome adversity."[50] In the case of proto-poch@ pop, the ability to "survive from whatever materials they have at hand" is a useful strategy for the "clandestine border crossing" into mainstream media.[51] The analogy of poch@ pop artists as migrant border crossers is further supported by poch@'s connection with the pochteca traveling merchant discussed in Chapter 5.

Just as *rascuache* might possess negative connotations dependent upon the context of the immigration topos, or rhetorical commonplace, Ramón Garcia problematizes the use of *rascuache*, which he describes as "camp." For poch@ pop, *rascuache* presents a method and framework for interpreting the reclamation of dominant symbols for decolonized messages. Garcia critiques what he views as a reductive aesthetic:

> It [rascuache] comes from the Chicano critics and artists that appropriate it and make it positive and unthreatening. For nobody wants to be *rascuache* in a material way, because it is simply a lack of resources and funds and it implies bad taste. After all, calling someone *rascuache* is an insult, in the same way that calling someone *Naco* is an insult; they are demeaning designations.[52]

Garcia's criticism responds to Tomas Ybarra-Frausto who writes that to be *rascuache* "is to posit a bawdy, spunky consciousness, to seek to subvert and turn ruling paradigms upside down."[53] Even though art critic Ybarra-Frausto brought the *rascuache* sensibility to the attention of Chican@ audiences, other scholars have similarly interpreted it as a strategy of resistance.[54] Although I would not reduce the diversity of poch@s artists in the U.S. to a single methodology, many of the poch@ pop artists perform methods supported by the theoretical rationale of *rascuache* methodology as they reclaim dominant symbols to redirect the power moving through these hegemonic symbols and productions. Gómez-Peña takes ownership

DOI: 10.1057/9781137498076.0007

over *rascuache* as he names it, although Alcaraz describes his methodology in similarly coded terms in Chapter 4.

Both Gómez-Peña and Alcaraz provide salient examples of poch@ pop because they self-identify with the trope of poch@. Still, there are pop culture producers who also demonstrate similar characteristics which seem to employ a *rascuache* approach. To return to film, Robert Rodriguez could be considered one of the most popular cinematic auteurs of Mexican heritage who has achieved mainstream success, though it was not always so. Charles Tatum's description of Rodriguez's early filmmaking mirrors the making-due-with-what's-at-hand strategy for survival:

> Robert Rodriguez made his film *El Mariachi* for less than $10,000, an incredible feat....he shot his streamlined and lean film in less than four weeks using very efficient production methods: he served as a one-person movie company fulfilled various artistic roles as writer, director, director of photography, sound recordist, and editor, as well as the labor-intensive roles of grip, gaffer, property manager, and co-producer.[55]

Despite the fact that Rodriguez has not called his early filmmaking style *rascuache* does not take away from his ability to circumvent the cost of mainstream cinematic productions with his "do-it-yourself" ethos. Amalia Mesa-Baíns explains that *rascuache*, or *rasquachismo*, is inventive and serves to maintain the dignity of the *rascuache* performer: "In rasquachismo, one has a stance that is both defiant and inventive...it is a combination of resistant and resilient attitudes devised to allow the Chicano to survive and persevere with a sense of dignity."[56] Inventive defiance possesses similarities with the subversive complicity of poch@ pop producers because both rely upon strategies and nontraditional elements of resistance in the service of those who cannot openly respond to all threats, stereotypes, and deficiency rhetoric.

Conclusion

This work builds upon previous work in which I focused on the intersection of pop culture and rhetoric.[57] I examined the rhetoric of what I broadly categorized as Mexican American hip hop through the analysis of the music by the Los Angeles hip hop fusion band Ozomatli. Specifically, I drew attention to how Ozomatli performs linguistic, epistemic, and musical-rhetorical border crossing that provokes cultural and social consciousness.

DOI: 10.1057/9781137498076.0007

Given their appointment as cultural ambassadors by the U.S. government, I focused on Ozomatli's navigation of dominant systems of power while performing music that subverts hegemonic policy and history. I point out how the mestiz@ hip hop draws from diverse musical traditions like *banda, cumbia, merengue, ranchera,* and others while addressing transnational social justice issues—some of the very same issues of immigration and inequality that self-identifying poch@ pop culture producers engage with and challenge. The importance of this study for *Reclaiming Poch@ Pop* was the identification of cultural *mestizaje,* mestiza consciousness, and mestiz@ rhetoric that stem from Anzaldúa's *Borderlands/La Frontera* and appeals to Latin@s and non-Latin@s in the U.S. One of the salient intersections that I noted between hip hop and what has been called mestiz@ rhetoric was Kermit Campbell's quote from Anzaldúa in *Gettin' Our Groove On: Rhetoric, Language, and Literacy For the Hip Hop Generation* about the connection between identity and language: "So, if you want to hurt me, talk badly about my language."[58] Even outside of discussions of rhetoric, notions from mestiz@ rhetorician Anzaldúa permeate investigations into pop culture. And *Reclaiming Poch@ Pop* is no different.

In the last decade, the representation of Latin@s in pop culture has changed, in large part because of the growing number depicting their realities. This book comes about at an interesting time for Latin@ pop culture. At the moment, there are multiple media sources that provide positive influences for the identity construction of the next generation of poch@ pop producers. This generation of pop culture consumers has the *Daily Show's* Al Madrigal and TV shows like MTV's *Washington Heights* (2013), *Latination* (2004–2014) and *American Latino* (2004–2014). On public radio, there are shows like Latino USA and Alt-Latino that address political and social issues impacting people of Latin American heritage. In addition, more media sources are following the model of Maria Hinojosa's Futuro Media, and the *Huffington Post* has a "Latino" section. Not to be outdone, Fox News Latino covers similar issues from the other side of the political aisle. Partnered with ABC and NBC respectively, Fusion and Mun2 demonstrate interesting partnerships by Telemundo and Univision to appeal to the English-speaking audience in the U.S. Also, HBO's documentary series *The Latino List* (2011) and *The Latino List: Volume 2* (2012) demonstrate a positive progression in the production and consumption of pop culture with the inclusion of contemporary role models like "Wise Latina" Supreme Court Justice Sonia Sotomayor.

DOI: 10.1057/9781137498076.0007

Diverse in content and identities, the sites of analysis for *Poch@ Pop* contribute to the texts by Latin@ that disrupt, contest, challenge, and resist the messages in media, politics, and policy that support systemic inequality. Poch@ pop lets you laugh when you want to cry, gives a collective middle finger, and mutters *"no mames"* to the legislators who write policy to police brown bodies and minds, doing their best to subjugate through frustration and heartbreak. But as the indigenous saying goes, humor heals, and poch@ pop embodies the heart of a revolutionary behind the clenched teeth smile in response to the question about "how to pronounce your name" or "you speak Spanish, right?"

Notes

1   Mun2 2012.
2   Anzaldúa 1987; Bhabha 1994.
3   Anzaldúa 1987, 77–78.
4   Anzaldúa 1987, 76.
5   Avila-Saavedra 2011, 274.
6   Sandoval 1999.
7   Villanueva 1993, 39.
8   Martinez 2009.
9   Hernández 2011.
10 Keller 1994; Mayer 2003; Noriega 2000; Ramírez-Berg 2002; Rodriguez 1999.
11 Amaya 2010, 806.
12 Avila-Saavedra 2011, 276.
13 Tatum 2001, 52.
14 Desi Arnez and Lucille Ball separated in 1960, although Ball first filed for divorce in 1944.
15 Nericcio 2007; Torres 2003.
16 Pimentel and Velázquez 2009.
17 Avila-Saavedra 2011, 272.
18 Hernández 1991.
19 Burke 1950, 503.
20 Gates 1988, 52.
21 Gómez-Peña 2000, 208.
22 Pérez 1999, 7.
23 Pérez 1999, xviii.
24 Aparicio 2003, 99.
25 Aparicio 2003, 101.
26 De los Santos 2012, 322.

DOI: 10.1057/9781137498076.0007

27   Baca 2008.
28   Baca 2008, 6.
29   Arizona Senate Bill 1070, or the Papers Please law, passed in 2012, which empowered local law enforcement to question anyone "suspected of being in the country illegally" and made it a misdemeanor for any suspected undocumented person caught not carrying legal documents.
30   Dickinson 2008, vii.
31   Amaya 2010, 802.
32   Anzaldúa 1988; Rodriguez 1983; Villarreal 1959.
33   Aldama 2009.
34   Deleuze and Guattari 1987.
35   See Cindy Y. Rodriguez's CNN article "Day of the Dead trademark request draws backlash for Disney" from Sat May 11, 2013 at http://www.cnn.com/2013/05/10/us/disney-trademark-day-dead 8 Sept 2013. Web.
36   Dickinson 2008, 3.
37   Thackara 2011.
38   Aldama 2002, 180.
39   Baca 2008, 11.
40   Baca 2008; Baca and Villanueva 2010.
41   *Pocho Handbook* 1980, 26.
42   Sahagún 1950, 21.
43   Townsend 2000, 195.
44   Gómez-Peña 2000, 47.
45   Hesford 1999, 4.
46   Pérez 1999, xviii.
47   Young 2004, 32.
48   Villanueva 1997, 183–184.
49   Fregoso 1993, 23.
50   Spener, 2010, 9.
51   Spener 2010, 9.
52   Garcia 1998, 214.
53   Ybarra-Frausto 1991, 155.
54   Broyles-González 1994; Gaspar de Alba 1999; Mesa-Bains 1999.
55   Tatum 2001, 73.
56   Mesa-Baíns 1999, 157–158.
57   Medina 2014b.
58   Anzaldúa qtd in Campbell 2005, ix.

DOI: 10.1057/9781137498076.0007

4

Alcaraz and Madrigal: Re-appropriating Poch@ for Resistance: A Time and Place for Poch@ Pop

Abstract: *In Chapter 4, I discuss the mainstream integration of poch@s such as Al Madrigal on the* Daily Show *to contest discourse about Latin@s. This chapter then focuses on selected political cartoons of Lalo Alcaraz. These pop culture producers subvert dominant colonial narratives that tokenize people of color in the media or exoticize people of color in political rhetoric. Further, this chapter specifically looks at how the art of* Pocho.com's *Lalo Alcaraz resists cultural deficit rhetoric by challenging policy portraying all Latin@s as potentially "illegal" (SB 1070), and racist in their education (HB 2281). Alcaraz's art demonstrates the kinds of subversive messages that appeal to the growing population of cultural producers and consumers.*

Medina, Cruz. *Reclaiming Poch@ Pop: Examining the Rhetoric of Cultural Deficiency.* New York: Palgrave Macmillan, 2015. DOI: 10.1057/9781137498076.0008.

DOI: 10.1057/9781137498076.0008

Living in Arizona during the passages of Senate Bill 1070 and House Bill 2281—legalizing racial-profiling of brown folk and outlawing Mexican American Studies (MAS) respectively—I participated in various marches, rallies, fundraisers, and community events against the bills. Human rights groups such as the United Nations publicly criticized SB 1070, although Arizona's system of legislation moved forward in an abusive exercise of dehumanizing power. Arizona legislatures enacted policy that is indicative of how such legislation materializes racist ideology supporting myths and projects of white superiority. Poch@ pop disrupts colonial and neocolonial discourse, interstitially challenging and subverting ultraconservative rhetoric. In the context of colonial narratives of Latin@ deficiency, the productions of poch@ pop culture filled the void on behalf of defiant Latin@ perspectives and voices that were silenced by media coverage of Arizona politics.

Though the political cartoons of Lalo Alcaraz—editor-in-chief of *Pocho.com*—will serve as the main sites of analysis, I begin with the poch@ pop of Alcaraz's *NPR Latino USA* and *Pocho.com* collaborator Al Madrigal. On the April 2, 2012 episode of the *Daily Show*, Madrigal's interview with Tucson Unified School District (TUSD) board member Mike Hicks demonstrates the logical fallacies of Anti-Ethnic Studies rhetoric. Madrigal's interview with Hicks about the banning of Tucson High School's Mexican American Studies program raised awareness about the ban and the flawed assumptions from which it operates for audiences who were not immediately familiar with the situation. This interview served as an important moment in the struggle against HB 2281 because it uncovers the colonial myths of white superiority undergirded by the portrayal of Latin@s as culturally deficient. In effect, the bill outlawed the pedagogy and curriculum that were designed to be culturally relevant because it challenged neocolonial myths of white supremacy.[1]

As a pop culture production addressing the debate over HB 2281, Madrigal's interview can be viewed as an effective rhetorical production communicated through a satirical genre. During Madrigal's interview with TUSD board member Michael Hicks, Hicks unknowingly revealed the prejudicial beliefs held by supporters of the ban, highlighting how banning education is a mechanism of colonial subjugation. Employing an exaggerated form of Socratic method, Madrigal's questions about the ban revealed that the bill only targets the Mexican American Studies (MAS) program even though other Ethnic Studies programs discuss

DOI: 10.1057/9781137498076.0008

similar issues of oppression. By dialectically asking questions about the other Ethnic Studies programs at Tucson High School, Madrigal prompts Hicks to explain that the Asian American, Native American, and African American studies programs are not the target of HB 2281. After some follow-up questions, Hicks agrees that African Americans learn about oppression when they study the history of the African American experience in the U.S. Still, Madrigal further exposes the ill-informed leadership of Tucson Unified School District when Hicks refers to "Rosa Parks" as "Rosa Clarks" in numerous instances. Although Hicks does not change his mind about the MAS program, Madrigal's rhetorical question-posing demonstrates the logical fallacies embedded in the outlawing of the MAS program.

More insidiously, Hicks voices the conspiratorial claims about the MAS program that have nothing to do with the curriculum. Madrigal paraphrases back to Hicks his claim that students feel "loyal to this guy [the teachers in the program] because he bought me burritos," to which Hicks responds in the affirmative "right."[2] Because of the genre of the *Daily Show* is satire, apologists for the ultraconservative policy claim that the interview was manipulated in order to entertain the audience, portraying Hicks as the focus of the humor derived from the segment. However, there is no sign of trick editing or voiceovers that do not match up with what is being said, no matter the context. In contrast with Madrigal's interview with MAS teacher Curtis Acosta, Hick's ethos and the ethos of the TUSD school board can be understood as working against their community by neglecting their purpose to educate. Madrigal's use of the Socratic method provides Hicks with figuratively enough rope to hang himself with. More broadly, Madrigal's *Daily Show* interview with Hicks epitomizes the fallacies transmitted in cultural deficiency rhetoric that reinforce colonial narratives and neocolonial policy.

Unfortunately, cultural deficiency rhetoric and the cliché stereotypes that support racist arguments have been transmitted in the majority of media representations, with very few opportunities for poch@ pop producers to challenge these misrepresentations. It is only recently with the *Daily Show* and Madrigal's segments that poch@ voices have taken center stage. In fact, Madrigal addressed the issue of representation on his first appearance in 2011 on the May 17 episode of the *Daily Show* in a segment titled "Aliens vs. President-Immigration Reform." Newly-appointed Senior (*pronounced señor*) Latino correspondent, Al Madrigal, meta-critically explained that President Obama's campaign pandered to

DOI: 10.1057/9781137498076.0008

the Latin@ population when addressing the issue of immigration reform. What makes Madrigal's criticism "meta" was that the logos structuring his message implicated the *Daily Show* and their hiring practices:

> [President Obama]'s had his whole term to do something about immigration and he's just bringing it up now. I mean that would be like, I don't know, having your own show for twelve years, hiring every race and religion and creed of correspondent under the sun—Indians, Brits, Blacks, two Canadians—then when the demographic numbers become completely unavoidable, you hope to make up for it by googling 'Mexican comedian' and *voila*.[3]

Madrigal's tongue-in-cheek critique of the very show that he is featured on highlights how poch@ pop culture producers subvert mainstream media despite their seemingly complicit participation in the very same media production. Through the genre of satire, Madrigal shows how the inclusion of Latin@s is attractive from a commercial standpoint while remaining a political threat: "The tension created by the contradictory response of the Anglo establishment to the U.S. Latin American community—commercially welcoming, but culturally rejecting—would continue to shape the development of the Hispanic audience."[4] Many might argue that there has been a lack of Latin@s desiring to take part in the media, but the careers of award-winning journalists such as Maria Hinojosa, who founded the Futuro Media Group and anchors Latino USA on National Public Radio, and Gustavo Arellano, editor-in-chief of the *Orange County Weekly* and syndicated "Ask a Mexican" columnist represent a tradition in varying media outlets that counters dismissive arguments about Latin@ desire to participate. Much like the artists who I identify as poch@ pop, Latin@ producers of culture in the U.S. carry the responsibility and burden of giving voice to the marginalization of the audiences they address and represent.

R. Jay Magill points out in *Chic Ironic Bitterness* that the use of satire by ethnic "Others" is a part of counter-hegemonic traditions of resistance in popular culture. Magill explains that the detachment and irony found in satire as "social resistance have been around in any number of American cultural productions for ages ... as well as in the works of countless artists and writers, all in need of a sort of psychic armor against a dominant political and commercial culture trying to smother existing ways of life."[5] As with many instances of satire, the message transmitted in the guise of humor possesses an unsettling logical foundation in statistical data. In Hector Amaya's analytical breakdown of the percentages of Latin@s

DOI: 10.1057/9781137498076.0008

in journalism, the lack of representation motivating Madrigal's comedic resentment towards Stewart is revealed in the alarmingly small percentages and fractions of percentages. He explains,

> In journalism, Latinos account for 4 percent of personnel in print news, and 6 percent of news staffers in English-language television (NAHJ, 2007). Bob Papper (2003: 21) has found that Latinos account for only 1.5 percent of radio newsstaffers and, in television, for only 4.4 percent of news directors. The lack of Latino personnel in news has a predictable effect on coverage. Federico Subervi's latest report on Latino representation in television news media shows that stories about Latinas/os account for only 0.82 percent in the major television networks and CNN (2005: 4).[6]

It seems clear why the work of Latin@ producers who continue to create pop culture employ resistant strategies like satire because of the marginal opportunities afforded to Latin@s by the media.

The subject and style of Madrigal's initial appearance on the *Daily Show* as immigration and the low percentage of Latin@s in the media is distinctly poch@. Though Madrigal does not reference poch@ in his *Daily Show* appearances, Alcaraz refers to Madrigal as an "all-around pocho" in *Pocho.com*'s YouTube content[7], and Madrigal appears as "Migrant Editor" on *Pocho.com*'s "About" page. The political cartoons of Alcaraz and *Daily Show* appearances by Madrigal exhibit the subversive strategy of humor that contribute to the " 'pocho aesthetic' that is rebellious and playful."[8] Because the *Daily Show* is clearly satire, the writers and producers are self-aware of the self-criticism that they bring to the attention of viewers. Still, the playfulness described by Dickinson underlies why Madrigal simultaneously jokingly embraces his token status while pointing out the broader issue of discriminatory hiring practices in the media.

A decade prior to Madrigal's appearance on the *Daily Show*, Alcaraz began creating his cartoon *La Cucaracha* in 2002, which was the first Latin@-themed syndicated political cartoon. More importantly to this discussion, Alcaraz was one of the first, if not *the* first, to not only self-identify as poch@, but also to name his website *Pocho.com* and his radio show the *Pocho Hour of Power*. In an interview with Univision, Alcaraz explains the conscious decision to embrace poch@: "A friend and me created *Pocho Magazine* back in the 80s and we took the word pocho and flipped it over and said, 'we're proud to be pochos.' "[9] It is telling of Alcaraz's unapologetic opposition to neocolonial paradigms characterizing poch@ as a deficient Latin@ identity, especially given the prevalent use of poch@ as a pejorative in the writing of canonical U.S. Latin@

DOI: 10.1057/9781137498076.0008

writers such as Richard Rodriguez and Gloria Anzaldúa. In *Hunger of Memory*, Rodriguez establishes the intersection between his improvement in English and the negative perception of him by other Mexican Americans. Poch@ functions as a trope justifying the poor treatment by family friends and people in Rodriguez's community as he improves in school and loses his ability to speak the Spanish language:

> *Pocho* then they called me...*Pocho*. (A Spanish dictionary defines that word as an adjective meaning 'colorless' or 'bland.' But I heard it as a noun, naming the Mexican-American who, in becoming an American, forgets his native society.).... Most of those people who called me a *pocho* could have spoken English to me. But they would not. They seemed to think that Spanish was the only language we could use, that Spanish alone permitted our close association...I felt that I had betrayed my immediate family. I *knew* that my parents had encouraged me to learn English. I *knew* that I had turned to English only with angry reluctance. But once I spoke English with ease, I came to *feel* guilty.[10]

Rodriguez describes poch@ as connoting a linguistic insecurity associated with a lack of Spanish-speaking ability, which is also read by family and friends as "pocho-Rodriguez" turning his back on his culture. Rodriguez not only captures the negative ethos of poch@ as a cultural traitor, but his experience also emphasizes the necessary level of resistance that Alcaraz performs by re-appropriating poch@ as a trope of agency.

Unfortunately, when *Hunger of Memory* was published, Rodriguez's experience also provided ethos for arguments against bilingual education. Concluding that the subtext of pathos in Rodriguez's experiences completely rejects bilingual education data exemplifies a non sequitur: this conclusion does not logically follow the premise. In *Bootstraps: From an American Academic of Color*, Victor Villanueva describes Rodriguez's rhetoric of assimilation while articulating the tension embodied by poch@ when he writes:

> Mexican Americans may have culture in common with many Mexicans, say, but Mexican Americans also have culture in common with fellow Americans. Their relation to the Mexican can become antagonistic when they favor the American inordinately, as in a Richard Rodriguez.[11]

Unlike poch@s who subvert dominant messages espousing assimilation issues such as English-only education, Rodriguez locates himself as singularly complicit in the colonial bootstrap narratives that champions

DOI: 10.1057/9781137498076.0008

the individual while dismissing the community and culture that helped the individual. Ironically, Rodriguez achieves recognition from within the Latin@ community by producing autobiographical writing about education while negatively impacting the education of Latin@s en masse. This discussion comes full circle when Frederick L. Aldama points out how Alcaraz's (2004) collection *Migra Mouse: Political Cartoons on Immigration* "takes shots at mainstream Latinos such as English-only proponent Richard Rodriguez,"[12] thereby evincing how poch@ pop artists produce discourse in opposition to colonial rhetoric of assimilation.

Unfortunately, the ideological resignation of Rodriguez serves as a kind of synecdoche, representing the experience of some Latin@s in the U.S. who believed assimilation without resistance was the only option. In a *Columbia Review of Journalism* article on Alcaraz called "No HABLA Español," Ruth Samuelson asserts that Alcaraz and his embracement of poch@ "was ahead of his time. *Pocho* is popping up everywhere these days, from Twitter handles to bands and performers."[13] But the rhetorical appropriation of poch@ was not always so. Even in Gloria Anzaldúa's "How to Tame a Wild Tongue," she describes the impetus for the use of poch@ stemming from its influence on language. However, Anzaldúa demonstrates greater nuance as she expounds on the colonial implication:

> "*Pocho*, cultural traitor, you're speaking the oppressor's language by speaking English, you're ruining the Spanish language," I have been accused by various Latinos and Latinas...Words distorted by English are known as anglicisms or *pochismos*. The *pocho* is an anglicized Mexican or American of Mexican origin who speaks Spanish with an accent characteristic of North Americans and who distorts and reconstructs the language according to the influence of English.[14]

For Anzaldúa, the reflection on her experience with poch@ does not substantiate compliance with dominant narratives, as in Rodriguez's *Hunger of Memory*. Instead, her life stories only display pathos and motivation for her conceptualization of a new mestiza consciousness, which refuses to operate within the binaries ascribed by colonial borders. Anzaldúa's new mestiza consciousness helps explain why an Univision interviewer can explain without cynicism that "many like Alcaraz have expressed pride in having both a Mexican and an American heritage asserting their place in the diverse American culture."[15]

Alcaraz's political cartoons, specifically those responding to recent legislation in Arizona, serve as sites of examination for this chapter on

DOI: 10.1057/9781137498076.0008

the subversive complicity—the ability to work within a system while working against it—in poch@ pop. The cultural productions elucidate the *rascuache* appropriation of dominant figures and employ the rhetorical strategy of humor to criticize ultraconservative laws and politicians. Ultraconservative politicians and policy reaffirm white superiority as SB 1070 and HB 2281 frame Latin@s as illegal, racist, anti-American, and, by default, culturally lacking. Simply stated, the appropriation of poch@ by artist like Alcaraz represents how the once pejorative term serves as a symbol of resistance by producers of Latin@ culture who challenge deficiency representations. Given Alcaraz's self-identification as poch@ with his *Pocho.com* news and satire website, and his *Pocho Hour of Power* radio show, the poch@ pop cultural productions of Alcaraz represent generative sites for examining the strategies of resistance to issues facing Latin@ audiences in the U.S. such as bilingual education, immigration, racial profiling, and attacks on ethnic studies.

Alcaraz, language, and the growing poch@ audience

The trope of poch@ in pop culture remains complicated because of the rhetorical strategies employed in messages, as well as the complex matrices of language in the U.S. Ruth Samuelson at the *Columbia Review of Journalism* is correct in proclaiming Alcaraz ahead of his time, in part because Alcaraz identified early on the growing population of pop culture consumers. Samuelson notes that Alcaraz's *Pocho Magazine*, which turned into *Pocho.com*, provoked audiences to question the assumptions in media while producing content for what would become poch@ pop consumers. Anabell Romero similarly notes that "[i]n their efforts to break common stereotypes about Chicanos [Pocho.com] became the pioneers of producing content in English and 'Spanglish', while all other Latino media was strictly in Spanish."[16]

Presenting data on the Latin@ audience in the U.S., América Rodriguez points to studies commissioned by Univision that highlight the deliberate attention given to language in consideration of their audience. As a Spanish-language media giant, Univision would naturally want to evaluate the viewership trends of Latin@s in the U.S.:

> Other Univision commissioned data reinforce the notion that the Hispanic market can no longer be defined as linguistically unitary. NHTI data show that just 31% of Hispanic households watch Spanish language television.

DOI: 10.1057/9781137498076.0008

However, these data also show that 69%, or more than two thirds, of Hispanic households, watch only English-language television.[17]

With language no longer a dominant indicator of Latin@ audiences in the U.S., it came as no surprise that Univision, in partnership with ABC, launched its English-language news station, Fusion, on October 28, 2013.[18] While Spanish-language network Telemundo has had a partnership with NBC dating back to 2001, the Mun2 network continues to offer only English-language content online via *Mun2.tv*.

To describe what poch@ pop producer Alcaraz has done as simply "appealing to Latin@s in the U.S. with entertaining subject matter" overlooks the complexity, contradictions, and subversive nature of Alcaraz's work, which creates a tension not readily replicable. In *Your Brain on Latino Comics*, Frederick Aldama maintains that Alcaraz "complicates the representational map" because he's not afraid to make Latin@s the subject of his humor: "The comic book's visual narrator and verbal narrator can work in tension or harmony, but their individual parts are taken up by the reader as a whole; this double narrator, along with the character narrator, can work to convey an ethnically conflicted storyworld."[19] Unlike scholars who critique the (mis)representations of Latin@s in mainstream cultural productions, Alcaraz blurs the line of stereotypical representation, strategically crossing lines of bourgeois expectations to draw attention to marginalized perspectives and issues. When he appropriates the messages from dominant cultural productions such as Mickey Mouse in *Migra Mouse*, he undermines the assumptions embedded in the image. The reader therefore has to be conscious of how the poch@ pop challenges the worldview represented by Alcaraz's use of dominant cultural symbols.

From a rhetorical perspective, poch@ pop such as the work of Alcaraz highlights the complex ideological interplay of humor and politics with pop culture productions. To analyze rhetoric is often to examine how power moves through communication, yet the strategic appeal of humor complicates power relationships because humor can transgress the rigidity of social constructs. While the trope of poch@ creates what Kenneth Burke calls a terministic screen that "directs the attention to one kind of field or another,"[20] humor strategically subverts assumptions and expectations of audiences across fields. Describing "pocho humor," Dickinson acknowledges the tension created by Alcaraz's political satire. She explains that "[c]ontemporary Chicano humor, in all its complexity, provides an important means of assessing the highly dialogized nature of

DOI: 10.1057/9781137498076.0008

contemporary Chicano discourse."[21] The dialogic nature of Chican@ and poch@ discourses might explain why Telemundo has been partnered with NBC for two decades, yet these mainstream media networks fail to garner poch@ audiences across the board.

Though the issue of language is often cited as the subject of commissioned studies, the fluid and shifting Chican@-ness and Latin@-ness, or *Chicanidad* and *Latinidad*, do not provide a fixed ideological baseline or terministic screen, through which media producers can appeal. A recent pop culture production that portrayed this spectrum of political and cultural consciousness was the Public Broadcasting Service (PBS) series *American Family* (2003) with Edward James Olmos and Esai Morales. The subject of *American Family* is a contemporary multi-generational family of Mexican heritage in Los Angeles that suffers the loss of the matriarch Berta, played by Sonia Braga. What makes the show a relatively accurate depiction of Latin@s in the U.S. is not the linguistic code-switching, discussions of mom's tortillas, or the old-world acoustic guitar soundtrack. Instead, Edward James Olmos as the curmudgeonly patriarch who is upset by the instances of Aztec dancers practicing in his home and youth painting murals on his barbershop walls accurately portray how Chican@ culture often competes with the conservative worldview of older generations. It should also come as no surprise that when Olmos' youngest adult son in *American Family* is shown typing at his computer, there is a *Pocho* magazine poster hanging on his wall. A series such as *American Family* depicts the spectrum of worldviews within a contemporary Latin@ family in the U.S., which might only be possible on PBS, where commercial budgets are minimal and viewership can be niche. At the same time, the broad reach of PBS stations dictates storylines that appeal to progressive and neoliberal audiences who could be offended by more subversive humor.

The tension created by conservative opposition to Chican@ consciousness and culture complicates appeals to this diverse audience of people with Latin American heritage in the U.S. Similar to Dickinson's identification of "pocho humor," linguist Carla Breidenbach examines the ideology of English, Spanish, and Spanglish use by Alcaraz's cartoon *La Cucaracha* to explain what she calls "pocho politics." Concerned with the connection between language and politics, Breidenbach looks at how Alcaraz "uses his comic strip *La Cucaracha* to enact his Chicano identity and political ideologies from within a post-Chicano (Wegner, 2007) Discourse, the combination I name 'pocho politics.'"[22] Breidenbach

DOI: 10.1057/9781137498076.0008

describes the linguistic code-switching, or going-between languages with the same sentence or utterance, by Alcaraz as a strategy "to enact his specific identity as a socio-political Chicano, his own special brand of 'pocho politics.'"[23] The work of both Dickinson with poch@ humor and Breidenbach with poch@ politics informs how poch@ pop can be interpreted as even transgressing elements of Chican@ ideology. Poch@ pop encompasses a complex matrices of language, ideology, politics, culture, and identity encoded in cultural production—the same matrix through which this generation of poch@ consumers interprets pop culture.

Rascuache methodology, poch@ humor and political tacos

This generation of poch@ consumers is savvy with regard to their awareness of pop cultural productions that extend their messages beyond clichéd representations or neoliberal celebrations of culture. Similarly, I approach the examination of the rhetoric of poch@ pop through a theoretical framework that poch@ artists categorize and describe in mainstream discussions of their work. As I mention in Chapter 3, Guillermo Gómez-Peña describes the methodology of his La Pocha Nostra troupe as techno-*rascuache*: "strategies of recycling and recontextualizing ideas, images and texts continue to be central aspect of our performance methodology."[24] Like poch@ pop performance artist Gómez-Peña, Alcaraz describes his method for production by saying that, "I create direct editorial cartoons and cutting-edge media manipulation art."[25] What Alcaraz calls "media manipulation" echoes the *rascuache* or techno-*rascuache* methodology that Gómez-Peña describes: both create their popular culture productions through a process of (re)appropriating and recycling available resources—oftentimes hegemonic symbols—which they invert to challenge the clichéd assumptions that portray Latin@ culture as deficient.

As a theoretical underpinning of *rascuache* methodology, Anzaldúa's a new mestiza consciousness has not only created space for this discussion, but her composing method also implies a *rascuache* approach. In *Toward a Mestiza Rhetoric*, Anzaldúa's description of her writing process in an interview with Andrea Lunsford evokes a *rascuache* process: "The act of writing for me is this kind of dismembering of everything that I am feeling, taking it apart to examine it and then reconstituting it or recomposing it

DOI: 10.1057/9781137498076.0008

in a new way."[26] Even though Anzaldúa does not use *rascuache* to identify her writing process, the method of dismembering and reconstituting possesses similarities with Alcaraz's description of his media manipulation. The rhetorical composing of media by Alcaraz demonstrates how poch@ pop producers perform *rascuache* methodology, often in the service of satirizing ultraconservative ideographs by using the ethos and pathos of the image against the ideology it represents.

Also discussed in Chapter 3, *rascuache* describes a strategic (re)appropriation which includes "resourcefulness and ingenuity allowing the oppressed to overcome adversity"[27] that scholars posit as a strategy of resistance.[28] Art critic Ramón Garcia points out that the very use of the term *rascuache* is in and of itself an act of (re)appropriation: "It [rascuache] comes from the Chicano critics and artists that appropriate it and make it positive and unthreatening. For nobody wants to be *rascuache* in a material way, because it is simply a lack of resources and funds and it implies bad taste."[29] The reason that many Chican@ pop culture producers have not crossed-over is that "taste" in pop culture could be explained as the evaluation of aesthetics according to the assumed habitus—expectations acquired through experience—by bourgeois, white middle-class audiences.[30] In a neocolonial context, the bourgeois measurement of aesthetics and appropriateness support colonial paradigms in which the subject of colonial power seeks to mimic the colonial standard, only to fall short of due to the fixed colonial binary.[31]

In productions of poch@ pop, a *rascuache* methodology espouses the ethos and spirit of resistance as an agenda beyond the primary purpose of entertainment. In his interview with Univision, Alcaraz explains his *rascuache* methodology as motivated by his desire to educate his audiences about social and political injustices through entertainment. Alcaraz describes what I term subversive complicity[32] as transmitted in his rhetorical "political tacos":

> I take issues like immigration and I try to explain it to people by flipping them around and also making them fun...I think everyone should be political, but not all people are going to be political, so I make little "political tacos" for everyone to enjoy once in a while and have a little snack and go, "oh yea, I understand what the DREAMers are" or "I understand why immigration is messed up."[33]

The "flipping" that Alcaraz performs with issues such as immigration highlights the *rascuache* method of (re)appropriation that inverts the

DOI: 10.1057/9781137498076.0008

hegemonic topoi of hot-button issues. Fortunately for poch@ audiences, they receive Alcaraz's messages without ingesting acerbic myths of white superiority that precipitate the revenge of Moctezuma.[34] Alcaraz's "political tacos" communicate messages relevant to Latin@ audiences without further propagating the internalization of colonial narratives.

The ethos of the *rascuache* methodology is that bawdy, spunky aesthetic that is perhaps best characterized by the rhetorical element of humor that poch@ pop producers deploy. The humor that Alcaraz includes in his satirical productions targeting Arizona politics make the consumption of his political tacos palatable for audiences with different worldviews, as demonstrated in the political cartoons of Alcaraz that serve as sites of analysis. Alcaraz's strategic use as humor is context-dependent because it "rebels against a range of norms... [and] the humor of those who feel caught between cultures can be defensive, work to construct new norms, and reinforce old prejudices."[35] Poch@ humor relies on the tensions from the assumptions that viewers bring to their reading of Alcaraz's work which tend to respond to specific political issues. Rhetorically speaking, humor depends on the notion of *kairos*, or the most effective moment for a given argument because humor can be defined as the wrong thing being said at the right time. Poch@ pop cultural productions rely upon the juxtaposition of the politically inappropriate in mixed company in order to provoke consciousness of issues that often go unmentioned in polite company.

The prejudice practiced in politics and represented in the media has a dialectical relationship with the poch@ producers who may play the essentialism game strategically if only to challenge the assumptions performed by these hegemonic apparatuses. Employing essentialism in humor can be tricky because superficial readings of stereotypes portraying Latin@s as lacking can reinforce beliefs of non-conscious audiences. Analyzing Alcaraz's use of language and "pocho politics," Breidenbach notes that "Alcaraz's strategy of resistance includes using stereotypes typically considered part of Mock Spanish and inverting them to shed an ironic light on them."[36] However, mainstream audiences can misunderstand the "satire, tricksters and irony" because these genre and strategies can be "missed altogether, particularly when the reader is contemplating such weighty topics as victimization and social justice."[37] Alcaraz's poch@ pop seeks to entertain, although the primary purpose of his social critiques can be difficult to separate from the irreverent humor he employs to appeal to apolitical audiences.

DOI: 10.1057/9781137498076.0008

Sites of analysis

The selections from Alcaraz's political cartoons that serve as sites of analysis for this chapter focus primarily on Arizona as the geopolitical context in the U.S.-Mexico borderlands where colonial myths of white superiority are revealed in state policy. Alcaraz addresses familiar rhetorical topoi, or commonplaces, of poch@ humor that "frequently address[es] immigration and its relationship to American nationalism; the under-and misrepresentation of Chicanos in U.S. media; and the traditional cultural markers of Chicano authenticity."[38] With the passing of Senate Bill (SB) 1070—allowing for the racial profiling of Latin@s who *may be* illegal—and the passing of House Bill (HB) 2281 that outlawed Mexican American Studies at Tucson Magnet High School, these topoi have had their rhetorical power amplified given the historical moment of *kairos* that these bills precipitate. As one who studies rhetoric while identifying as Latin@, Chican@, and poch@, I find the power moving through the discourse of SB 1070 and HB 2281 indicative of enduring colonial and neocolonial ideologies in the policy of ultraconservative legislation. It is for this reason that I identify these cultural productions by Alcaraz—both because they embody the characteristics and methodology of poch@ pop. Moreover, these cartoons were created dialectically, offering, as it were, Socratic responses by Alcaraz to the fallacies corroborated and manifested into laws controlling Latin@ bodies and minds.

Pop culture productions provide sites for articulating responses to the controversy around SB 1070 and HB 2281 outside of political debates, while simultaneously providing modes of documentation. The positive effects on students' lives as depicted in the documentaries *Precious Knowledge* (2011) and *Outlawing Shakespeare: The Battle for the Tucson Mind* (2013)—not to mention graduation rates and state tests scores[39]—stand in direct opposition of cultural deficiency rhetoric that continues to accuse Latin@s of *not caring about education.* Cultural deficiency rhetoric continues to serve as justification for cutting resources and programs because political discourse frames Latin@ students as lacking, thereby justifying systemic inequality. In 2008 American Enterprise Institute (AEI) and 2012 American Council on Education (ACE) reports, Latin@ students were described as "lagging" behind graduation rates of their White counterparts. In the November 28, 2012 issue of *The Chronicle of Higher Education,* Sara Lipka's article "As Minority Students' Completion Rates Lag, a New

DOI: 10.1057/9781137498076.0008

Report Asks Why" discusses the 2012 ACE report by further perpetuating the deficit discourse of these reports. Though the agendas of the AEI and ACE reports can be debated, the purported purpose of these reports was to draw attention to the institutional need for more resources to be placed on the retention of Latin@ students. However, the perpetuation of discourse such as "lag" to compare Latin@s to their White counterparts demonstrates the enduring myth of non-Whites as at a cultural and racial deficit, rather than the victims of systemic inequality.

Signed into law in April of 2013, Arizona's SB 1070 took on greater meaning as an ideograph of ultraconservative politics championed by groups like the Tea Party that employ the ethos of the Constitution for their political agenda backed billionaires like the Koch brothers.[40] The police state political cartoon by Alcaraz is archived in the "Portfolio" section of his personal website Laloalcaraz.com. The overt message conveyed by the image is that Arizona, as a state, has been replaced by a red "Police" state. The term "police state" possesses connotations entrenched in historical contexts where fascist regimes overtook governmental power in an all-encompassing capacity, deconstructing systemic oversight of checks and balances. The cartoon captures Alcaraz's poch@ pop ethos as it communicates a critical argument about the politics, rhetoric, and legislation of the state of Arizona.

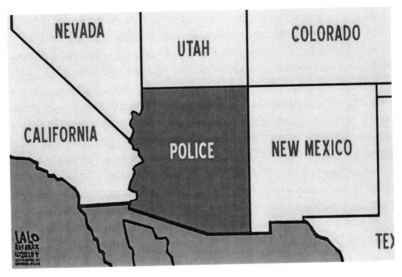

FIGURE 4.1   *Police state*

DOI: 10.1057/9781137498076.0008

Instead of lodging accusations such as "fascist" against the power in Arizona, Alcaraz simply colors the state red so as to make the connection between the ultraconservative politics of the state and the heightened enforcement of Latin@s in the context of SB 1070. Given Alcaraz's positionality as a political commentator, he could be categorized as being in the fourth estate of the press that provides oversight of governmental proceedings, although his poch@ sensibilities and the perspective he brings blur this taxonomy, allowing him to speak from a more objective fifth estate. In the past, this kind of identification might sound accusatory; however, the current state of news media demonstrates the role of ideology in the communication of political coverage, with media channels like Fox News and MSNBC positioning themselves in opposition to one another down conservative and progressive party lines.

The racist ideology of the neocolonial agenda becomes vibrantly illuminated in the context of Arizona's law that calls into question the citizenship of all Latin@s by casting doubt on the legal status of all brown bodies in the state. In a piece about HB 2281, Henry Giroux explains that:

> [Race] is either coded as a style, a commodity, or devalued as a criminal culture and defined as a threat to a supposedly under-siege white, Christian nation…race is more and more erased as a political category and reduced to the narrow parameters of individual preference, psychology or prejudice. Privatizing race preserves the dominant power structures that produce modes of structural racism that extend from racial discrimination to racial exclusion practiced by schools, governments, banks, mortgage companies and state policies, among others.[41]

By enacting a law that positions non-whites as potentially "illegal," Arizona maintains not only its conservative power structure but also it reified myths of white superiority into law. Perhaps if the very same "grassroots" ultraconservative organizations like the Tea Party, backed by billionaires like the Koch brothers, were not simultaneously casting doubt on the citizenship of President Barack H. Obama—the first black president—the repetition of the rhetorical attack would be less overt. In an infamous Associated Press (AP) photo taken of Arizona Governor Jan Brewer with President Obama on an airport tarmac, Brewer is either pointing or shaking her finger at the current POTUS. In the context of race, Brewer's gesture can be read as not only a scolding gesture of disrespect, but also as an exercise of white privilege against the first African American president.

DOI: 10.1057/9781137498076.0008

Unfortunately, Brewer's defiant pose is not an image taken out of the political context of Arizona. Returning to Alcaraz's cartoon of Arizona, his choice in the use of the image of Arizona plays on the ultraconservative politics, which the state represents. The state name and image possess particular rhetorical power as an ideograph of right-wing politics and worldviews. However, as a poch@ pop rhetorical production, the message communicated by Alcaraz's visual rhetoric subverts and challenges the message of Arizona imagery. This visual production of Alcaraz embodies the *rascuache* method of recycling and re-contextualizing available means of persuasion. In an analysis of Alcaraz's *Migra Mouse*, Aldama acknowledges the deliberate rhetorical decision-making that Alcaraz performs by choosing racist quotes about his cartoons for his book cover. Alcaraz does so to respond to these messages while appropriating their arguments to contribute to his ethos by demonstrating the worldviews that his productions subvert. Aldama points out that "[c]learly, Alcaraz chose to put these misreading on the jacket cover to show how racism can prevent a reader from recognizing a narrative blueprint that uses devices and signposts to satirize contemporary society as well as to poke fun at identity politics generally."[42] In line with poking fun of identity, I move to Alcaraz's satire of Maricopa County's Sherriff Joe Arpaio, who runs his campaign by touting his tough on crime platform.

Dated 2010 in the top right corner of Alcaraz's "Sheriff Joe: America's Top Hop" political cartoon, the political satire was produced during the same year as the passing of SB 1070. In effect, SB 1070 and its facilitation of racial profiling further supported Arpaio's office which already coordinated immigration raids in Maricopa County. Never shying from media attention, Arpaio's portrait in his Sheriff attire is a part of his "tough on immigration" political campaigns that have won him a record six four-year re-elections in the conservative county of Maricopa, where Arizona's state capital of Phoenix is located. The political position of sheriff as an elected office also epitomizes the public opinion of non-Latin@ voters in Arizona who believe in colonial narratives of the Wild West, and regard Arpaio as a kind of John Wayne character who brings law to the hallucinatory bandito borderlands of the ultraconservative collective unconscious. For Maricopa voters and conservative fans, Arpaio is John Wayne in John Ford's *The Searchers* (1956), tracking down his niece to kill her because her whiteness has been "soiled" by the Native Americans who kipnapped her. Audiences and voters accept the sacrifice of lives and human rights when it is depicted on screen by Wayne and cowboys in white hats because it reflects their particular, albeit twisted, worldview.

DOI: 10.1057/9781137498076.0008

FIGURE 4.2   *Sherriff Joe: America's Top Hog*

DOI: 10.1057/9781137498076.0008

As with the rhetorical decision-making to color Arizona red above, Alcaraz lampoons Sheriff Joe Arpaio with a cartoon image that draws rhetorical efficacy from the similarities with the original. The poch@ pop *rascuache* method of Alcaraz strategically transforms elements of Arpaio's physical features to resemble those of a pig, drawing on the popular slang of "pigs" to describe police. Yet, Alcaraz's political satire of Arpaio is more complex than name-calling. Arpaio's self-promotes as the nation's "toughest cop" because of the degrading pink uniforms that he has inmates wear at his notorious "tent city" in the Arizona heat that averages between 95–106 degrees from the months of May to September. The original image from which Alcaraz's production is derived comes from Arpaio's own political campaign and serves as an ideograph for the voters who have re-elected Arpaio despite lawsuits accusing him of human and civil rights violations. On October 3, 2013, Reuters reported that Federal District Judge Fred Murray Snow ordered the appointment of an independent monitor and a community advisory board for Sheriff Joe Arpaio after finding that his office engages in racial profiling of Latin@s.[43]

The news of an overseer mandated by federal judge Snow seems like a small concession for Arpaio considering the allegations of racism, illegal immigration enforcement, and misuse of funds against him that precipitated his oversight. The case of Arpaio brings to light the importance of pop culture as a space for political discourse. The coverage of activism and public outcry against Arpaio remains by and large marginal in mainstream media outlets when compared to nightly programming dedicated to celebrity news. A simple Google News search on October 20, 2013 of the terms "Joe Arpaio racial profiling" yielded 591 results compared to 3,380 results generated from a search using the terms "Sofia Vergara Latino," a popular Latina actor from the television show *Modern Family*. A more broad search on the same day using the terms "Joe Arpaio" and "Sofia Vergara" yielded 6,850 for Arpaio compared to the 36,000 results for Vergara, with the complication that Arpaio's political ties link him to political stories while Vergara's attention mainly stem from publicity related to pop culture promotion. By no means does this kind of informal quantitative research demonstrate a conclusive causal relationship. Instead, by drawing comparisons between politics and sensational news spectacles, informal comparisons between these news genres exemplify the need for poch@ pop cultural productions that make instances of colonial and neocolonial oppression entertaining and, therefore, more

DOI: 10.1057/9781137498076.0008

consumable, despite the relatively fractional media coverage these topics represent.

Much like the need for poch@ pop that SB 1070 demonstrates, the opposition to Arizona HB 2281 has benefited from pop culture interventions. Soon after SB 1070 was passed in Arizona by Governor Jan Brewer, House Bill 2281 was also enacted. Written by former State Superintendent of Public Education, Tom Horne, and enacted by his successor, John Huppental, HB 2281 outlaws classes deemed to be anti-American, segregating by race, promoting resentment among races, and overthrow of the government. While the logic of the policy written by ultraconservative policymakers appeals to neoliberal audiences as well as conservative audiences, the implied subject of HB 2281 that is never named is Tucson Magnet High School's Mexican American Studies (TUSD MAS) program. Below is an image that Alcaraz produced, showing the Ethnic Studies program represented by a book at this burned by the flames of the house bill.

As a response to Arizona's ban on Ethnic Studies, specifically Mexican American studies, Alcaraz produced multiple cartoon images with the Tucson Ethnic Studies debate as the subject matter. The image "Ethnic Studies 2281" produced by Alcaraz does not seem to perform the rhetorical strategy of (re)appropriation as in other cartoons; it still appeals to audiences by satirizing the law as a form of reactionary book-burning. The book burning cartoon typifies Dickinson's description of pocho humor as rebelling "against a range of norms, from standard English/ Spanish languages rules to such concepts as 'All American' and 'puro Mexicano'... [which is why] the humor of those who feel caught between cultures can be defensive."[44] Furthermore, Alcaraz's image of Ethnic Studies metaphorically burning in the flames of HB 2281 alludes to the burning of Pre-Columbian codices and texts by the Europeans during the Conquest of the Americas.[45]

In another example of Alcaraz's criticism of HB 2281, the image of Arizona painted white exhibits the characteristics of *rascuache* poch@ pop as it makes a biting critique about the role of race in the Tucson Ethnic Studies debate. Similar to the political cartoon of Arizona as a red state, the image is the visual representation of Arizona, however, in the process of being painted white or "whitewashed." The northern edge still remains distinctly darker for contrast while the southern edge drips, and a bucket of white paint, or whitewash, labeled "Arizona Ethnic Studies Ban" sits open below it. Still wet with whitewash, the ban is freshly

DOI: 10.1057/9781137498076.0008

FIGURE 4.3   *"Ethnic Studies"*

DOI: 10.1057/9781137498076.0008

FIGURE 4.4   *"Whitewashing Arizona"*

imposed with the 2010 date written in the upper right hand corner below Alcaraz's signature. In some ways more subtle than the image of book burning, the racial component that Alcaraz forefronts and exteriorizes what is often ignored in mainstream discussions of the controversy with the metaphor of white-washing. Although the Ethnic Studies program was started as a result of a federal desegregation ruling, proponents of HB 2281 fail to recognize the irony in their allegations of racism against the program because it separates students by race.[46] The omission of race by mainstream media coverage demonstrates what Victor Villanueva laments about race in the U.S.: "racism—the idea and even the word—is becoming more taboo than politics and religion as subjects for casual conversation."[47] Ignoring the role of race supports the functioning of colonial paradigms that controls racialized bodies through socially constructing narratives which reinforce ideologies situating non-white people as lacking—inside and outside the context of the Tucson Ethnic Studies debate. By ignoring race, white privilege continues to be protected and avoids becoming the subject of public inquiry.

DOI: 10.1057/9781137498076.0008

Humor and satire provide a few rhetorical strategies to challenge and potentially transgress the discursive power of what public policy validates and condemns. Alcaraz's work manifests what Dickinson asserts about poch@ humor in the genre of satire when she explains that "satire is used to urge Chicanos to reject Anglo American values in favor of Chicano or Mexican values."[48] Even though Dickinson's assertion about the purpose of the rhetorical use of satire holds validity, I would complicate this explanation by pointing out that the agenda of the Mexican American Studies program in concert with African American and Pan-Asian programs was to represent the diversity of the state and U.S. Still, the rejection of Anglo values is salient in the case of educational policy that privileges European history in Advanced Placement courses, while outlawing Mexican American history that positively impacts graduation rates and state test scores.[49]

Conclusion

As someone who lived in Tucson and worked down the street from Tucson Magnet High School, I witnessed firsthand how the positive efforts and activism of students and teachers in the Mexican American Studies (MAS) program. The MAS program presented curriculum that was relevant to the lives of students, and the program effectively subverted a system of education that mainly serves to institutionalize Latin@ students. The community activism of students and educators against the oppressive system of Arizona education should ultimately be celebrated as a success because the struggle for education is a part of a larger tradition that will continue.[50] As an enduring pop culture production, Al Madrigal's report on the MAS program for the *Daily Show* highlights the absurdity of unchecked colonial narratives in a way that only through satire is possible. In a conversation with the TUSD teacher Curtis Acosta, who was also a subject of the segment, he told me that out of all of the media coverage of the MAS banning, by networks like CNN and many local news organizations, the *Daily Show* was actually the most thorough when it came to fact-checking the statements Acosta made following the interview.[51]

The examination of contemporary poch@ pop productions reveals how neocolonial rhetoric continues to subjugate Latin@s in the U.S. In Chapter 5, the connection between contemporary poch@ pop and

DOI: 10.1057/9781137498076.0008

colonial conquest becomes more apparent through the layered messages embodied in the work of Guillermo Gómez-Peña and collaborators who produced a modern re-imagining of a Pre-Columbian codex. Answering the call of rhetorical scholars Damián Baca and Victor Villanueva to draw on Pre-Columbian rhetorical ways of knowing in the study of contemporary Latin@ topics,[52] the next chapter draws on the Nahuatl etymology of poch@ to provide greater historical context of contemporary poch@ pop productions.

Notes

1 Medina 2013a.
2 Madrigal 2012.
3 Madrigal 2011.
4 Rodriguez 1997, 288.
5 Magill 2007, ix.
6 Amaya 2010, 806.
7 Interview from *Pocho.com*. YouTube. (http://www.youtube.com/watch?v=KdiZHUKkBwI) January 3 2012.
8 Dickinson 2008, vii.
9 Romero 2013.
10 Rodriguez 1982, 29–30.
11 Villanueva 1993, 57.
12 Aldama 2009, 25.
13 Samuelson 2012.
14 Anzaldúa 1987, 77–78.
15 Romero 2013.
16 Romero 2013.
17 Rodriguez 1997, 298.
18 Wood 2013.
19 Aldama 2009, 26.
20 Burke 1966, 50.
21 Dickinson 2008, viii.
22 Breidenbach 2012, 210.
23 Breidenbach 2012, 211.
24 Gómez-Peña 2000, 47.
25 Alcaraz 2009, 204.
26 Lunsford and Ouzgane 2004, 44.
27 Spener 2010, 9.

DOI: 10.1057/9781137498076.0008

28 Broyles-González 1994; Gaspar de Alba 1999; Mesa-Bains 1999; Ybarra-Frausto 1991.
29 Garcia 1998, 214.
30 Bourdieu 1977.
31 Bhabha 1994.
32 Medina 2013a; 2013b; 2014a; 2014b.
33 Romero 2013.
34 Moctezuma II was the Aztec emperor who met with Hernan Cortes, and who punished those who were unaccustomed to the endemic chemicals of Mexican tap water, according to urban legend.
35 Dickinson 2008, 3.
36 Breidenbach 2012, 218.
37 Gutierrez-Jones qtd. in Dickinson 2008, 45.
38 Dickinson 2008, viii.
39 Cabrera et. al 2012.
40 Mayer 2010.
41 Giroux 2012.
42 Aldama 2009, 29.
43 Schwartz 2013.
44 Dickinson 2008, 3.
45 Serna 2014.
46 Horne 2010, 1.
47 Villanueva 2006, 114.
48 Dickinson 2008, 9.
49 Cabrera et. al 2012.
50 Cabrera, Meza, Romero and Rodriguez 2013.
51 Acosta 2012.
52 Baca and Villanueva 2010.

5
Poch@teca: Re-understanding the Historical Trajectory of a Proto-Chican@ Identity

Abstract: *Chapter 5 traces the etymological connection between poch@ and pochteca by examining the traveling merchant role of the pochteca that crossed territories and spoke in the tongue of the foreign territory. The historical origin of poch@ outlines a salient re-understanding that provides context for the contemporary reclamation by poch@ pop artists. As the site of analysis, Gómez-Peña's collaborative* Codex Espangliensis *provides a generative demonstration of how the integration of historical tropes resists colonial rhetoric about Latin@s in popular culture, drawing on Mesoamerican literacy practices. The visually-oriented text brings the conversation full circle by looking at comic-like representations that critically juxtapose mainstream pop culture icons like Mickey Mouse with images from the Conquest of the Americas.*

Medina, Cruz. *Reclaiming Poch@ Pop: Examining the Rhetoric of Cultural Deficiency*. New York: Palgrave Macmillan, 2015. DOI: 10.1057/9781137498076.0009.

Poch@ pop culture and deficiency rhetoric

In a performance piece by Guillermo Gómez-Peña, his character El Aztec High Tech transmits a radio broadcast introduction to his *New World Border* performance, noting "I'm here with Super-Pocho Dos, *el vato más loco de Pacoima...*"[1] Gómez-Peña's use of the character Super-Pocho Dos is noteworthy because it echoes his use of the trope poch@ for his theater troupe La Pocha Nostra. Gómez-Peña challenges and subverts negative discourses and rhetoric with his playful mix of Pre-Columbian references—El Aztec High Tech—and the reclaimed poch@ trope, responding to and playing on the beliefs, values, and assumptions of his audiences. Poch@, as earlier noted, has pejoratively signified a Latin@ cultural traitor.[2] In dialogue on stage, El Aztec High Tech and Super Pocho Dos visually mirror the *rascuache* refashioning of the concepts of poch@, Aztec, and technology in a way that responds to the perceived deficiency regarding Latin@ culture.

The Super-Pocho moniker in tandem with El Aztec High Tech show how the anglicized Latin@ and tech savvy identities are included in the multiplicity of Latin@ identities, demonstrating the epistemological trajectory of poch@ pop. This chapter draws on Pre-Columbian rhetorical productions to help explain how the crossing over into mainstream pop culture and subverting ideological borders by poch@ pop producers is a part of a larger historical tradition in the Americas. To demonstrate this tradition, I look at the Nahuatl origins of the word poch@, which provides additional historical context. These connections illuminate shared rhetorical strategies of the Pre-Columbian pochteca traveling merchant class and those employed by contemporary poch@ pop artists during ideological border crossings.

In this chapter, I examine Gómez-Peña's collaboration with Enrique Chagoya and Felicia Rice on the *Codex Espangliensis* to demonstrate how Pre-Columbian rhetorical traditions inform the rhetorical elements and strategies of poch@ pop producers. The *Codex Espangliensis* has been regarded as a visual pictographic production that incorporates pop culture icons such as Mickey Mouse and Superman in a recreation of the Conquest of the Aztecs, complete with Aztec warrior imagery, as well as a contemporary mestiz@ re-imaging of a Pre-Columbian codex.[3] I find myself in a dialog with Damián Baca as I follow his call for rhetoricians to "confront the pictographic writing of pre-Columbian Mexican civilizations in meaningful ways."[4] I examine the *Codex Espangliensis* as

DOI: 10.1057/9781137498076.0009

crossover pop culture production by poch@ artist Gómez-Peña, and I posit that the Pre-Columbian epistemology and ways of knowing represented by the codices inform the rhetorical resistance of contemporary poch@ pop producers.

In *Mestiz@ Scripts, Digital Migrations and the Territories of Writing,* Baca argues that mestiz@ codex rhetoric displace assimilation.[5] However, poch@s are often regarded as those who are the most assimilated, yet their pop culture includes cultural relevance that challenge the cultural erasure of assimilation, from which globalizing industry benefits. I build on Baca's work and draw from both rhetorical and popular cultural studies to reveal a more nuanced understanding of poch@ by tracing the Pre-Columbian knowledge represented in the *Codex Espangliensis.* In doing so, I draw attention to the rhetorical strategies revealed by Pre-Columbian epistemology that possess import into the discussion of pop culture as resistance to cultural deficiency in the context of recent anti-Latin@ legislation.

Gómez-Peña's incorporation of Pre-Columbian visual rhetorical traditions as a self-identifying poch@ artists provokes further examination of the interplay between the rhetorical strategies of the Aztec pochteca traveling merchants and the strategies employed by poch@ pop artists. By embracing the trope of poch@, Gómez-Peña's work with Aztec literacy creates a tangible link between Pre-Columbian knowledge and poch@ resistance. Building on the Pre-Columbian rhetorical productions of visual literacy, Gómez-Peña, Chagoya, and Rice critically respond to the anti-Latin@ propositions in California. More than a decade later, this pop culture as critical response has political import to our current historical moment when similar ultraconservative legislation targets the rights of Latin@s in Arizona, Alabama, Georgia, Indiana, South Carolina, and Utah.[6] Through their discursive production, these laws rhetorically de-authorize the knowledge and legal presence of Latin@s in the U.S.

Some of the most well-known modern mentions of poch@ in writing by Latin@s in the U.S. express the tension that the writer experiences when made to feel not quite Mexican and not quite American. As discussed earlier, both Richard Rodriguez and Gloria Anzaldúa provide important context surrounding the use of poch@ as a linguistic trope indicative of cultural identity. This chapter investigates poch@'s potential etymological connection with the Nahuatl pochteca because the root meaning of poch@ reveals a rhetorical wealth of symbolic resistance for artists who embrace poch@. The rhetorical uncovering of poch@ that

DOI: 10.1057/9781137498076.0009

I propose—by way of its etymological root—was inspired by William Nericcio's inquiry into stereotypes in popular culture, using the example of Speedy Gonzalez to recognize simulacra, or representations of representations that do not accurately portray the original subject.[7] Regarding poch@ as a potential simulacrum, or at least a floating signifier, poch@'s dominant meaning as the connotation "cultural traitor" appears to play a regulatory role in the authorization of a constructed cultural ideal. I examine poch@ in the historical and etymological context to show how poch@'s cultural traitor meaning does not relate to its Nahuatl root and why poch@ pop producers perform rhetorical strategies of the pochteca.

Pochoism, poch@s, and bi-culturalism

Gómez-Peña's rhetorical incorporation of Spanglish and Spanish in his performances underscores the close association of the poch@ trope with language. In perhaps the earliest scholarship on poch@, William E. Wilson's "A Note on Pochismo" identifies "pocho" as the root word of pochismo. Naming pochismo as a translingual variation of Mexican Spanish with Anglicized words that mirrors what has more contemporarily been called Spanglish, Wilson explains:

> Pochismo, derived from *pocho*, an adjective which originally meant discolored, has now come to mean a type of popular slang in Mexico. In the ever-growing list of *pocho* expressions are many hybrid words, artificial combinations of English and Spanish.[8]

Wilson's translation of poch@ as "discolored" corresponds with the Royal Academy of Spanish's definition of poch@ as "*descolorido, quebrado de color*"[9]; yet, this Spain-based dictionary fails to account for an etymology beyond modern meanings. A former colonial power in the U.S., Spain continues to uphold colonial superiority by omitting indigenous root words. While Wilson ignores the colonial implications of poch@ from a Mexican national perspective, he speculates that "*pochismo* seems destined to receive wider acceptance,"[10] speculating on the proliferation of the linguistic variance based on its popularity south of the border. However, the definition "discolored" denotes a deficient characteristic indicative of the linguistic difference of Mexicans in America and around the US-Mexico border.

DOI: 10.1057/9781137498076.0009

For mainstream audiences, the U.S.-Mexico border has come to represent a metonymy for impurity, violence, and other assumptions that justify the ill-treatment in the material world. Nericcio's post-modern deconstruction of Orson Welles' *Touch of Evil* (1958) problematizes the positionality of Latin@s in the U.S., especially when considering the U.S.'s collective gaze toward Mexico. Nericcio indicts the film as "attempt[ing] to answer this fundamental question of what it means to speak Mexican...to enact a scenario wherein the very fabric of Latina/o stereotypes is woven and unravels."[11] Nericcio's examination of *Touch of Evil* reveals essentialized notions of the border and the mestizo half-breed who is a result of the cultural contact zone at the historical moment when poch@ proliferates as a pejorative on the lips of Spanish speakers in the U.S. and Mexico. Considering the pop culture audience, Nericcio offers an indictment of the demand of "the reassuring logic the stereotype 'Mexicans' and 'Mexican Americans' provide for a U.S. critical community enchanted with diversity and difference as aesthetic categories, not material, breathing realties."[12] Neoliberal U.S. audiences reassure themselves that they can celebrate diversity without having to engage in cross-cultural practices, although pop culture provides that interstitial space where poch@ pop producers can play upon the essentialized notions embedded in racist metonymy. Poch@ pop artists strategically appeal to the assumptions of audiences to subvert their expectations as they (re)appropriate tropes and other meaning-bearing symbols.

That the stereotypes which Welles builds upon in *Touch of Evil* are so easily understood by U.S. audiences highlights the space in hegemonic logic that these cliché's occupy. This deficiency rhetoric about Latin@s rings as almost common sense for the viewing public; however, the construction of Latin@ identity in the U.S. at the same time of *Touch of Evil* reveals how these narratives became "the ways in which we people of color conduct ourselves in response to the ethnocentricity which has its roots in a colonial history, [or] internal colonialism."[13] Like Villanueva, I acknowledge that the popularity of "internal colonialism" came from Franz Fanon;[14] however, the representation of the U.S. Latin@'s loss of language and culture is salient in José Villarreal's 1959 novel *Pocho*.

In the bildungsroman *Pocho*, U.S.-born teenager Richard Rubio comes into conflict with his Mexican immigrant parents, especially their skepticism of education's ability to improve the lives of their American-born children. The bi-cultural experience of Richard causes him to experience a sense of schizophrenia that other authors[15] discuss as a part of

DOI: 10.1057/9781137498076.0009

the process of coming into consciousness as a Latin@ in the U.S. *Pocho*'s immature, adolescent protagonist Richard speaks from a naïve, non-community-oriented perspective in an argument with his father: "I have to learn as much as I can, so that *I* can live…learn for *me*, for *myself*—Ah, but I cannot explain to you, and you would not understand me if I could."[16] Richard's youthful resistance and lack of community-minded goals contribute to the discussion of the poch@ ethos as rejecting cultural community in favor of education. As Richard becomes older, he speaks of his "hunger to learn" eventually turning to the subject of his culture even though the young Mexican immigrants regard him as "a traitor to his 'race.'"[17] Factors of adolescent psychology and identity development are complicated by issues of gender, culture, and language. At the same time, it is worth noting that within polemics regarding assimilation, the story of *Pocho* is often viewed through a reductionist either/or narrative. Ultimately, Villarreal's *Pocho* underscores oppositional consciousness and deficiency rhetoric within the Mexican American community as the only options within a colonial paradigm. *Pocho* demonstrates two important issues related to poch@ pop: first, infighting within the Mexican American community comes as a result of destructive, internalized colonial narratives meant to turn community members against one another; second, the poch@ subject possesses a desire for education that compels him to learn about his culture, not reject it.

One of the most widely-read texts that include discussion of poch@ is Richard Rodriguez's *Hunger of Memory*. Discussed in different fields of English studies,[18] Rodriguez's conservative positions on English-only language policy exemplify what the trope of poch@ signifies, labeling him as an "obliging colonial agent."[19] Beginning on page one, Rodriguez identifies with the character of Caliban, the native subject who is marginalized and corrupted as he experiences colonialism in William Shakespeare's *The Tempest*. Rodriguez signals the self-awareness that he experiences as he idealizes and mimics the colonizers. For Rodriguez, poch@ serves as a signifier for both his regret and rejection, interwoven into his pro-assimilation message: "Most of those people who called me a *pocho* could have spoken English to me. But they would not. They seemed to think that Spanish was the only language we could use, that Spanish alone permitted our close association…I felt that I had betrayed my immediate family."[20] For Rodriguez, the trope of poch@ represents his inability to communicate in Spanish and loss of personal connection, which becomes conflated with accusations of his betrayal to his family, friends, and community.

DOI: 10.1057/9781137498076.0009

Published several years after Rodriguez, Gloria Anzaldúa writes about her experience as having been rejected by Latin@s who called her "pocho."[21] Like Rodriguez, Anzaldúa describes feelings of rejection associated with poch@ in *Borderlands/La Frontera*; however, Anzaldúa focuses on poch@ to contest colonial narratives, history, and knowledge through strategic uses of language. She complicates the interplay of language and identity by approaching the trope of poch@ with the attention of a linguist: "The *pocho* is an anglicized Mexican or American of Mexican origin who speaks Spanish with an accent characteristic of North Americans and who distorts and reconstructs the language according to the influence of English."[22] While Anzaldúa's writing is anything but dry scientific discourse, her treatment of poch@ demonstrates the blurring of linguistic boundaries that she performs in much of *Borderlands/La Frontera*. Drawing on English, Spanish, and Nahuatl, Anzaldúa embraces this cultural mestizaje, which she then demonstrates by adding epistemic layers to her writing with Pre-Columbian figures/tropes/imagery such as Coatlicue, Tlilli, Tlapalli, and Nepantla. Anzaldúa illuminates how indigenous ways of knowing can inform contemporary formations of identity and resistance to hegemonic knowledge and culture. The influence of *Borderlands/La Frontera* can be seen in the *Codex Espangliensis* vis-à-vis the blending of indigenous imagery with U.S iconography and critical text.

Pre-Columbian poch@ pop

Gómez-Peña's integration of Pre-Columbian history, knowledge, and culture in *Codex Espangliensis* awakens cultural memory that disrupts colonial narratives in the context of poch@ pop. Poch@ pop productions resist, contest, and subvert dominant narratives about Latin@s, often by (re)appropriating hegemonic symbols and employing them against dominant systems of power. Without the cultural memory of Pre-Columbian history, deficiency rhetoric becomes the dominant narrative that dismisses the literacy and cultural artifacts produced in the Americas before contact with Europeans. Evaluating Pre-Columbian literacy as a unique locus of enunciation, Baca explains that the codices were produced on what was called *amoxtli*, or "the pictographic manuscripts which served in the transmission and performance of *Huehuetlatolli*, a Nahuatl expression for ancient word and wisdom of the

DOI: 10.1057/9781137498076.0009

elders."²³ Unfortunately, the modern historical trajectory of the trope of poch@ is characterized by colonial standards of comparison, primarily via language, which—ultimately by design—frames the colonial subject as lacking. Earlier, rhetorical scholar Villanueva traces the roots of cultural deficiency rhetoric to the linguistic theories arguing that the children from supposedly "deficient" cultures should be regarded as having no language.²⁴

Pre-Columbian culture provides not only additional epistemic context, but it also contributes to decolonial approaches for the examination of contemporary pop culture. Consequently, Pre-Columbian ways of knowing reveal strategies in the sites of resistance where poch@ has been reclaimed as a trope of empowerment. I categorize Gomez-Peña's work, such as the *Codex Espangliensis*, as poch@ pop in part because of his performance artist troupe's name, La Pocha Nostra. I also consider it poch@ pop because of how Jennifer González describes the resistant strategies in the introduction of the *Codex Espangliensis*: "[Rice's typography weaving with] texts from Gómez-Peña's performance through and around the visual play of Chagoya's rhetorically sophisticated collages."²⁵ Gómez-Peña, Rice, and Chagoya appropriate pop culture icons to critically challenge historical narratives about Latin@s that resurface in anti-bilingual education policy in California at the time of the codex's production.

Gómez-Peña's written contribution to *Codex Espangliensis* maintains his performative flair and includes the switching between languages for the purpose of unsettling his audiences with the bi-cultural experience, an experience embodied in the excerpted "Free Trade Art" and "Chicanos: Radio Nuevo Orden." For poch@ pop producers, language can be indicative of culture and provide a pejorative context for the connotation of poch@ as speaking Spanish poorly or with Anglicism.²⁶ The colonial standard of language, evidenced through writing, upholds the colonial narratives constructed by colonials to subjugate the colonized, defining historical knowledge as the production of hegemonic history by way of colonially-sponsored fictional narratives.²⁷ The interplay of Aztec and pop culture imagery in the *Codex Espangliensis*, therefore, performs a visual disruption of the normalized historical representations of the Conquest as an act of imposing an enlightened civilization on a people without culture, literacy, and, by "logical" deduction, knowledge.

Vocal opposition is a tactic best employed in activist rallies and marches, although the message of resistance is not one that is easily

DOI: 10.1057/9781137498076.0009

consumable in pop culture mediums. In this next section, I follow the etymology of poch@ to the Mesoamerican figure of the pochteca to show how the crossover strategies of poch@ pop producers stem from an enduring historical tradition. At the same time, the rhetorical elements of the pochteca provide valuable insight into production of poch@ pop. After doing so, I turn to poch@ pop artist Gómez-Peña's collaboration on the *Codex Espangliensis* to examine the ways in which poch@ resistance is expressed through Pre-Columbian visual rhetoric by (re)appropriating dominant pop culture icons in a *rascuache* method.

Deficiency rhetoric and poch@ pride

The omission of attention paid to the culture of the Americas is indicative by its absence by and large in pop culture, though it is similarly alarming how Western rhetorical traditions focuses narrowly on the Greco-Roman tradition as the singular point of origin. Within the last decade, LuMing Mao has complicated how rhetorical scholars like George Kennedy have evaluated comparative rhetoric. Mao points out that Kennedy measures rhetorical traditions against the Western canon, and in doing so, demonstrates how these traditions ultimately fall short. Mao describes Kennedy's approach as reinforcing deficiency rhetoric by evaluating a culture's rhetorical tradition as "a 'deficiency' model—where one particular culture (read as non-Western) is determined to be lacking a concept of rhetoric or, worse still, a rhetorical tradition."[28]

The cultural deficiency model, which Villanueva and Mao identify, illuminates the implied logic in arguments about Latin@s lacking an epistemic rhetorical tradition. This assumption naturally omits visual spatial rhetorical productions, namely the codices that evidence not only a tradition of literacy, but also a complex oral rhetorical tradition. When examining poch@ pop that integrates Pre-Columbian literacy and visual rhetoric, poch@ pop raises awareness of traditions that have been erased by dominant historical accounts. In *Moctezuma's Mexico*, Mexican American anthropologist David Carrasco illustrates how the recognition of culture through the study of Pre-Columbian artifacts serves as a disruption of the colonial narrative:

> I was feeling both intense pride and cutting shame at my Mexican ancestry...I realized I had been taught that Mexico was a country valued only for its defeats, jokes and folklore but not for its civilization. These messages

DOI: 10.1057/9781137498076.0009

repeated aggressively and subtly, had registered in me as a Mexican American the conviction that ancestral dignity came from the civilized Romans, Greeks and even the Egyptians.[29]

Carrasco describes how the internalized narrative of Mexican history, culture, and knowledge had negatively impacted his identity, juxtaposing his experience with Pre-Columbian cultural artifacts as empowering him to reject deficiency narratives. The use of history to heal traumatic pasts is what Yolanda Leyva advocates for communities of color because they "have begun finding ways to reclaim and use history in order to restore our humanity and to recover from the devastation of our traumatic past."[30] Leyva echoes Inés Hernández Ávila's explanation that history *"es una gran limpia"*; however, Leyva recognizes the generative power of history as a site of cultural identification and reconciliation. By closely examining the history of poch@, I contextualize the rhetorical power of Pre-Columbian history and knowledge that undergirds the agency exhibited by contemporary poch@ pop.

I expand the etymological discussion of poch@ by decolonizing the Aztec pochteca from the paradigm where colonial narratives shape the discourse about authenticity, language, and cultural standards. Before arriving at the root pochteca, I begin with the complex manifestations of poch@ in the U.S. Even in the poetry of Américo Paredes, from the late 1930s, his use of poch@ complicates the negative connotations described in Jose Villarreal's novel *Pocho*, Richard Rodriguez's *Hunger of Memory*, and Gloria Anzaldúa's *Borderlands/La Frontera*. In "Reassessing Pocho Poetics: Américo Paredes and the (Trans)national Question," B.V. Olguin points out that as early as the late 1930s and 1940s, Américo Paredes challenges the pejorative use of poch@. Translated from Spanish, Paredes' poem is as follows:

I'm pocho! May God make me
the pride of the pochos
just as the pochos are my pride.
I would like to become
the pride of the pochos.[31]

Olgiun describes Paredes' celebratory poch@ poem as handwritten in Spanish, having never been published, which seems to speak to both the subversive nature of poch@ pop and the strategic disguising of the Pre-Columbian pochteca discussed at length later. Still, Paredes' early "pocho pride" demonstrates how the trope is divergently deployed in Spanish-language poetry prior to Villarreal's *Pocho*.

DOI: 10.1057/9781137498076.0009

The role of language adds severity to Paredes' proto-Chican@ deployment of poch@, especially compared to Villarreal's bildungsroman that portrays a young man perceived as a "traitor to his culture." Increasing with severity, the trope of poch@ mutates from a Mexican influenced by Anglo culture in Pocholandia to someone who turns their back on Mexican culture entirely. While time and space certainly seem to impact the severity of the pejorative, tracing the roots of poch@ back even further uncover historical connections with the pochteca,³² a social class of Aztec traders that spoke multiple languages, crossed into foreign territories, and gathered information for their home communities.³³ This chapter, therefore, examines poch@'s etymological connection with the Nahuatl pochteca, as well as the implications of this connection. The link between poch@ and pochteca dispels the floating signifier and simulacra of poch@, while additionally providing historical context that undergirds contemporary self-identification with poch@ by resistant pop culture producers.

In stark contrast to the knowledge recovered in Pre-Columbian rhetoric, recent legislation in Arizona provides an example of how Latin@ history and culture have been regarded in the material world. Following the passage of Arizona Senate Bill 1070, which sanctioned the racial-profiling of Latin@s, Arizona passed House Bill 2281 that outlawed Tucson Magnet High School's Mexican American Studies (MAS) program. Accused of promoting racism and anti-American sentiment, the MAS program incorporated Pre-Columbian tropes into the pedagogy and curriculum of the courses. Founded on the Mayan concept of "In La Kesh," and translated into the poem in Spanish as "*Tu eres mi otro yo* (you are my other me)" by proto-poch@ pop artist Luis Valdez, the classes followed sequences embodied by the Aztec figures of Tezkatlipoka, Quetzalcoatl, Huetzilopochli, and Xipe Toltec, which represent topics and themes of self-reflection, beautiful knowledge, the will to act, and transformation, respectively.³⁴

How the case of Tucson's MAS program relates to poch@ pop and the *Codex Espangliensis* is twofold: first, the *Codex Espangliensis* came about as a response to similar anti-Latin@ California propositions as Arizona's SB 1070 and HB 1070 targeting the bodies and minds of Latin@s. Second, reactionary policy demonstrates a perceived threat from Pre-Columbian history and culture to some Latin@ and non-Latin@ audiences—perhaps because it disrupts the safety of colonial narratives—though more likely because of its unapologetically critical view of projects of inequality in the Southwest that reinforce hegemonic systems of power.

DOI: 10.1057/9781137498076.0009

Poch@ and Pochteca

At the same moment when Luis Valdez's film adaptation of his play *Zoot Suit* (1981) gained critical attention, the trope of poch@ continued to be regarded with much disdain, as evidenced in Rodriguez's and Anzaldúa's reflections on poch@. Still, in a quasi-extension of Américo Parades' work, the *Pocho Handbook*, the collective anonymous writers of Pocho Cultures Research and Development propose a conceptual resolution for the rejection of those labeled as poch@s. The Pocho Cultures Research and Development begin to do so by first recognizing the negative connotations associated with the trope. The *Pocho Handbook* acknowledges that:

> Of the three Southwest cultural variations, of Mexican American, Chicano and Pocho, the now dormant Pocho has always been the most irreverent and controversial. What the Pocho has done or said in the past, combined with his poor way of doing and saying it, has continually provoked ridicule and resentment to what has been taken as the Pocho's attack on what is cherished and established Mexican tradition.[35]

Within the taxonomy prescribed above, those identifying as "Mexican American" fall into a more conservative, assimilationist ideology, while a "Chicano" would be someone identifying with more of a Mexican nationalist perspective. Regarded as a controversial identity, "pocho" is charged with rejecting, and even in some cases, attacking Mexican culture. And it is not without merit.

In *Hunger of Memory*, Richard Rodriguez's perspective demonstrates this pejorative construction of poch@. This is especially evident when Rodriguez argues that bilingual-education proponents "do not realize that while one suffers a diminished sense of *private* individuality by becoming assimilated into public society, such assimilation makes possible the achievement of *public* individuality."[36] Rodriguez's pro-assimilation message and rhetoric of individualism provokes the ridicule and resentment of Chican@s addressed in the *Handbook* because a Chican@ consciousness resists assimilation and recognizes the role of community in the development of individuals, which individualism rhetoric dismiss. In Rodriguez's writing, language plays a significant role in causing his family and friends to refer to him as pocho.

Discussed in Chapter 2, the ideological boundaries ascribed by self-identifying tropes can be similarly recognized in the categories used to

DOI: 10.1057/9781137498076.0009

taxonomize films made by Latin@s in the U.S. As rhetorical scholarship of the Americas exposes, Pre-Columbian knowledge and culture provide a larger historical trajectory for conceptualizing contemporary Latin@ epistemology;[37] additionally, for poch@ pop, Pre-Columbian rhetoric adds additional levels of complexity when examining the layers of power moving through the discourse in the cultural productions by Latin@ pop culture producers in the U.S. Continuing with the example of poch@ (re)appropriation in the *Pocho Handbook*, we see how Mesoamerican history and cultural memory interrupt the borders drawn by the ideologies of self-identifying tropes mentioned above.

As in the rhetorical strategies of poch@ pop artists, the collective Pocho Cultures Research and Development decolonize the trope of poch@ through the etymological connection and historical reference to the Pre-Columbian pochteca. The anonymous writer of the *Handbook* asserts that, "The Pocho are the rightful voice of our people in this land...and they were the rightful voice in the days of the ancient Aztecs."[38] The text draws on cultural memory of shared history in order to establish ethos with regard to the differences between Poch@s and Chican@s: "But as the Chicano becomes the new Aztec or the reborn Aztec, so the Pocho, as your namesake, becomes the new Pochteca or the reborn Pochteca."[39] The *Handbook's* connection between poch@ and pochteca possesses similarities with the scholarly discussion of the etymology touched upon in chapter three and in this hermeneutic exploration. Despite the *Handbook's* relatively simplistic explanation, the *Handbook* connects the pejorative connotation of poch@ with the visual rhetoric embodied by the Pre-Columbian pochteca, which Bernadino de Sahagún outlines in his sixteenth-century account, the *Florentine Codex*.

Interestingly, the visual rhetoric expressed in Pre-Columbian codices comes into focus with the work of Gómez-Peña, though the rhetorical power of Gómez-Peña's poch@ pop production can be better understood in the context of the pochteca in the *Florentine Codex*. The strength of the interplay of metaphor is further supported by the etymology of pochteca, which connects to geographical place. James Lockhart traces the origins of pochteca to the meaning "inhabitant of Pochtlan," relating to a trade group pre-dating the pochteca.[40] In the same vein, Robert Townsend traces the root of pochteca still further, and reveals a clearer connection with the contemporary "pocho":

> The term pochotl, from which pochteca and Pochtlán derive, was the same for the Bombax ceiba, the towering, sheltering tree of the tropical forests,

DOI: 10.1057/9781137498076.0009

which was traditionally regarded as a sacred "tree of life." In a figurative sense, pochotl means father, mother, governor, chief, or protector.[41]

Denotatively, the sacred "tree of life" meaning of pochotl affirms a literal connection that is consistent with the contemporary "bruised fruit"[42] meaning of poch@. The etymological link between pochteca and poch@ is strengthened by the shared pochotl—tree of life—root.

Wilson's translation of poch@ as "discolored" corresponds with the Royal Academy of Spanish's definitions,[43] which lacks an etymology beyond modern meanings. The absence of a root Latin or Greek term by the Royal Academy of Spanish can more than likely be attributed to the fact that poch@ comes from pochteca.[44] Additionally, the "father, mother, governor, chief, or protector" speaks to the inclusivity and transitive of the poch@ pop artists, with the "@" symbol, representing the "a/o" inclusivity of Chicanas and Chicanos.[45] Not only is the etymological connection between pochteca and poch@ poignant because of the rhetorical strategies embodied by Aztec traveling merchants, but also because pochteca provide a transformative symbol for pop culture producers self-identify as poch@. Poch@ producers serve as "protectors" in pop cultural contact zones by responding to ultraconservative policy and dehumanizing rhetoric.

Films such as the adaption of Javier Hernandez's comic book *El Muerto* into *The Dead One* (2007) represent problematic attempts at incorporating Aztec mythology into the popular cinematic genre despite the generative potential of this history. Valderrama, a Latin@ actor more widely known for his portrayal of the foreign-exchange character Fez in *That 70s Show* (1998–2006), earnestly portrays the part of the young man enslaved by the Aztec god of death. However, in much the same way that many Native American mythologies and religious ceremonies are represented as quasi-superstition by skeptical detectives in the cinematic adaptation of Tony Hillerman's novels, the Aztec imagery and Nahuatl language in *The Dead One* provide little more than a supernatural narrative device. Perhaps the grain of salt with which audiences approach these films has to do with what actually endures about Pre-Columbian Nahua history, culture and literacy coming from texts written by a Franciscan friar participating in colonization during the conquest of the Americas.

Re-inscribing history from the codices

Despite the emergence of Pre-Columbian rhetorical traditions in scholarship and interstitial pop culture sites, the resistance of poch@

DOI: 10.1057/9781137498076.0009

pop remains relatively disconnected from narratives in the mainstream discourse. While important attention has been paid to how the codex incorporates "strategies of resistance encoded in Mestiz@ cultural symbols... [and] as resistant rhetoric that addresses the larger backdrop of colonial subjugation and resistance in the Americas,"[46] I am similarly concerned with current neocolonial projects of oppression. The wake of recent ultraconservative legislations targeting Latin@s provides a historical lens that shades how the codex responds to contemporary subjugation of Latin@s. In Gómez-Peña's artist statement for the *Codex Espangliensis*, he describes the motivation for the project as paralleling similar attacks on Latin@s in the U.S.:

> [W]e were to produce a "post-Columbian" codex in response to the great Mexican crisis in California. Throughout the early '90s, a series of legislative propositions attacking immigrants and the Spanish language were being placed before the voters of the state, while federal immigration policies were being changed in sinister, draconian ways.[47]

Gómez-Peña refers to the "draconian" policy of California such as Proposition 187, which sought to bar undocumented children from attending public schools and to require healthcare providers to verify legal status before providing non-emergency care. Prop 187 and its predecessor Prop 209, which outlawed affirmative action in California, possess unsettling similarities with Arizona's SB 1070 and HB 2281.

The outlawing of Mexican American Studies in Tucson, Arizona, serves as motivation to re-examine and re-understand the historical influence of Pre-Columbian culture on contemporary media produced by poch@s for poch@s. Poch@ pop rhetorical responses to ultraconservative policy inspire me as a researcher because policy such as Arizona HB 2281 offer a model for anti-Ethnic Studies bills such as Texas's Senate Bill 1128, which would make college courses in Mexican American and African American Studies not count toward graduation. Ethnic Studies program scare ultraconservative systems of power because these programs challenge the myths of white supremacy in the Southwest.[48] When analyzing pop culture, these programs call attention to films that portray Latin@s as maids, thugs, banditos, gang members, or highly-sexual "fiery" Latinas.[49] Additionally, social justice education presents Latin@s with alternative representations of the indigenous in the Americas, rather than the colonial message that "natives need to be civilized" as in Mel Gibson's (2006) *Apocolyto*.[50]

DOI: 10.1057/9781137498076.0009

In order to attain crossover success, artists and pop culture producers require media attention for their work to reach commercial audiences. In a similar, if not somewhat reductive, sense, much of what is known about the Pre-Columbian Americas has been mediated through the documentation of the Nahua people, history, and culture by colonial researchers. The question of mediation and authorship from ancient periods is not unlike speculation about whether Plato accurately documented Socrates or if the Socrates in Plato's dialogues is in fact Plato's creation. For the ancient populations of the Americas, the mediation therefore cannot be attributed to a deficiency or lack of literacy practices present before the Conquest. Instead, the elimination of Pre-Columbian codices and cultural productions was a direct result of the colonial project of conquest that attempted to erase the knowledge and traditions of the indigenous.[51]

Bernardino de Sahagún, a Franciscan friar participating in the conversion campaign of indigenous persons to the Catholic religion, documents Nahua culture beginning in 1545 for what would become the *Florentine Codex: General History of the Things of New Spain,* which he revised until his death in 1590.[52] The *Florentine Codex* serves as not only a canonical historical text about the Nahua, but it also provides an account of the social, political, and professional role of the pochteca in Book Nine, the etymological root for poch@. Cynthia Kristan-Graham attests to the significant role of the pochteca disguised merchant in Nahua society, reiterating that Sahagún "devoted one of 12 volumes to merchants, or pochteca in Nahuatl. Since only two other volumes concern specific social groups—rulers and gods—Book 9, The Merchants attests to the importance of pochteca in Aztec society."[53] Furthermore, Sahagún's discussion of the disguised merchants' fluid social identity and their application of language and knowledge of other cultures demonstrates tactics that poch@ pop artists continue to employ.

In the *Florentine Codex,* Sahagún discusses the social class of the pochteca, of which the "Tzinacantlan" or "disguised merchants" were a part. Rhetorical strategies become evident when Sahagún discusses how the pochteca disguised themselves to cross over into neighboring territories:

> And behold, [as to] those known as [and] hence called disguised merchants: when the merchants went into Tzinacantlan before the people of Tzinacantlan had been conquered, to enter so that they did not look like Mexicans, in order to disguise themselves, they took on the appearance of the [natives]. As was the manner of cutting the hair of the people of Tzinacantlan . . . just so did the

DOI: 10.1057/9781137498076.0009

merchants cut their hair to imitate them. And they learned their tongue to enter in disguise.[54]

Often regarded as disguised merchants, the pochteca performed transactions with the inhabitants from other territories, mimicking their appearance and speech in order to build capital. The performance of linguistic diversity, depending upon audience, demonstrates the embodied rhetorical practices that Sahagún identifies as strengths and abilities.

The Mesoamerican traveling merchants perform strategies as cross-cultural agents that parallel the rhetorical work of poch@ pop producers. The pochteca gathered goods and information because of their ability to adapt to both the appearance and language of other territories. Sometimes spoken of as spies,[55] the pochteca shared the information and knowledge they gathered from other territories:

> And when they came to reach their homes, thereupon the disguised merchants sought out the principal merchants; they discussed with them the nature of the places they had gone to see. Accurately did they set forth their account of all that had happened there.[56]

The pochteca demonstrate a community-oriented ethos that poch@ pop artists share. Poch@ pop artists like Gómez-Peña and Alcaraz serve as cultural arbitrators, mediating news about political (in)action to both Latin@ and non-Latin@ audiences in the U.S.

In *The Nahuas After the Conquest*, James Lockhart describes the close-knit community of the pochteca within the larger structure of the Nahua society. Lockhart writes, "Merchants (*pochteca*; sing., *pochtecatl*)...[i]n the *Florentine Codex*, the pochteca are seen as a prominent group with their own tight organization and their own subculture."[57] As a subculture, entrance into this group would require knowledge about the merchant trade, as well as the necessary fluency of languages and cultural difference. The decision to enter into this subculture relied upon a shared belief in knowledge-building, including language acquisition and cultural competency. Although Lockhart dismissively summarizes Book Nine as focusing "on the group's ceremonial aspects and political connections than on its economic activity and internal organization,"[58] he fails to account for is the hermeneutic potential of indigenous ceremony as a rhetorical site interconnected with political systems of power.[59] The entertainment aspect of ceremony further illuminates how the ancient pochteca figure adds epistemological depth to the understanding and implications of the political and ceremonial work done by poch@ pop.

DOI: 10.1057/9781137498076.0009

Rhetorically speaking, the sophist is the Greco-Roman figure most closely paralleling the crossing of territories and spreading knowledge of the pochteca. Like the trope of poch@, sophists were much maligned by Greek rhetors. Victor Villanueva points out that the sophists suffered because of colonialism and their "outsider" status:

> The sophist themselves were the victims of a colonialism. We know that the first sophists were *metics*, immigrants to Athens from colonies in Sicily. And we know that among the reasons for the end of sophistry as honorable was xenophobia, a distrust—maybe even a hatred—of foreigners, including those who were citizens by way of colonialism.[60]

Although Villanueva analogizes the sophist for the scholar of color as foreigner in the field of rhetoric and composition,[61] it is important to keep in mind that the sophists—much like the pochteca—had to be rhetorically savvy to identify with audiences from differing ideological backgrounds.

The scholarly attention paid to the pochteca highlight characteristics that reveal rhetorical strategies employed by poch@ pop artists, even though poch@ pop producers may not be cognizant of the pochteca origins. As I will now discuss in greater detail, Gómez-Peña's collaborative *Codex Espangliensis* presents a message that is subversive in its depiction of the history taught in the U.S., while the integration of pop culture icons like Mickey Mouse and Superman contributes to the *rascuache* aesthetic that borrows from familiar artifacts, even as the familiarity ultimately unsettles.

Poch@ in "popular" Pre-Columbian culture

This chapter suggests that Pre-Columbian representations of rhetorical resistance are important to current concerns with popular culture in part because of the historical tradition from which they manifest. History and pop culture have many intersections, despite the reductive interpretation of pop culture as something ephemerally popular during a given historical moment—as though once it is identified as popular it ceases to be pop culture. In a more generous hermeneutic of pop culture, poch@ identity and cultural authenticity has played out historically between artists and scholars. Responding to Octavio Paz's disparaging views of poch@ identity, Américo Paredes discredits the "pocholandia" described by Paz as espousing colonial rhetoric of cultural deficiency:

> *Pocholandia*, as we all know, is supposed to begin in the northern Mexican states, extending northward into the southwestern United States... And it has

DOI: 10.1057/9781137498076.0009

not been viewed any more sympathetically from the south than it has from the north. The *pocho-pachuco*, with apologies to Octavio Paz, is not so much a creature hiding behind a mask as a poor soul wedged between the pyramid and the skyscraper.[62]

As a Latin@ in the U.S., Américo has a more nuanced view of the bi-cultural experience compared to Paz's essentialized "either/or" colonial paradigm that poch@ pop artists disprove and undermine. Complicating Parades' claim, I assert that poch@ pop artists create and negotiate the interstitial space between the pyramid and the skyscraper—with a foot in both worlds—though it is not the "creature" of Paz's colonial Other-ing.

The symbols of the pyramid and the skyscraper provide visual imagery that communicates messages through the juxtaposition of the contemporary and ancient. In the introduction of the *Codex Espangliensis*, Jennifer González aptly describes the blending of visual and written languages as producing an effect for the viewers so that they begin "to experience the dissonance of bi-cultural literacy as a concrete, material practice of reading in two paradigms."[63] Analyzing the *Codex Espangliensis* as a "mestiz@" codex, Baca interprets "such symbolization as a resistant rhetoric that addresses the larger backdrop of colonial subjugation...and displace the dominant historical narrative of cultural assimilation through continuous symbolic play with pairs, doubles, corresponding expressions and twins."[64] Just as the connection between the poch@ and pochteca demonstrates shared rhetorical elements, further examination of Pre-Columbian rhetoric of the Americas possesses potential for this generation of pop culture consumers and producers raised in Pocholandia.

My attention came to the *Codex Espangliensis* through Baca's *Mestiz@ Scripts, Digital Migrations, and the Territories of Writing* which marks one of few studies of the rhetorical practices of the pre-Columbian Americas. Making meaning from marginalized epistemologies requires a generative strategy of interpretation, and Baca skillfully draws on Pre-Columbian tropes and culture through what he describes as "enact[ing] a strategy of invention between different ways of knowing."[65] Extending the field of rhetoric and composition by bringing in Mesoamerican rhetorical traditions allows for "writing between worlds," inventing different ways of knowing using tropes grounded in the epistemology of Pre-Columbian literacy practices.[66] Turning his analytical lens on the *Codex Espangliensis*, Baca posits that it creates a new strategy for writing:

> By fusing and embellishing Mesoamerican pictography into European inscription practices, Mestiz@ codex rhetorics promote a new dialectic, a

DOI: 10.1057/9781137498076.0009

new strategy of inventing and writing between worlds...This revisitionist codex fuses multiple writing systems and languages including Aztec pictography, alphabetic *Nahuatl*, twentieth-century Castilian, Chicano iconography, Spanglish, and English.[67]

In addition, the *Codex Espangliensis* provokes important questions about Pre-Columbian intersections with contemporary poch@ pop producers, by exemplifying how this rhetorical tradition facilitates critiques of neocolonial policy. This examination is further undergirded by the moment of *kairos* provoked by the ultraconservative policy of Senate Bill 1070 in Arizona, empowering law enforcement to act as immigration agents. SB 1070 functions as a neocolonial apparatus that forefront dehumanizing binaries of "legal" and "illegal" as rhetorical questions indicting Latin@s in the U.S. by association.

Artists often respond to issues in the public consciousness and zeitgeist, and in the case of poch@ pop, the pochteca as the subculture on the vanguard testify to the historical tradition of rhetorically responding to oppositional threats. In *The Aztecs of Central Mexico*, Frances Berdan focuses on chapter five of Book Nine of the *Florentine Codex* and the assertions of power deployed by the pochteca in service of their communities. Berdan draws attention to the diversity within the pochteca class of merchants, interpreting what Sahagún calls the "vanguard merchants" as being a part of the "disguised merchants." Sahagún writes that when Moctezuma's message is not well-received, he declares war with the vanguard merchants going to the lead, appointed by the principal merchants with the disguised merchants following orders "wherever war was to break out."[68] Speaking to the quasi-celebrity status of pop culture producers in contemporary society, Berdan describes the pochteca as: "[t]hese professional merchant groups enjoyed distinctive privileges and a special status in the Aztec state. Merchants were important politically: They entered enemy territory as spies, they could declare and engage in wars, and they could conquer communities."[69] Interpreting the pochteca as a larger group of merchants made up of smaller subgroups allows for a more complex understanding of a fluid social class of merchants whose numerous identities parallel the numerous expressions, manifestations and interpretations of not only contemporary *latinidad*, but also the diversity of pop culture producers and productions.

As a revisionist pictographic codex, the *Codex Espangliensis* opens back to front with the binding on the right side, thereby challenging Western literacy practices of reading left to right. I support Baca's

FIGURES 5.1A AND 5.1 B *"Superman; Mickey sacrifice"*

DOI: 10.1057/9781137498076.0009

explanation that the layout of the pictographic frames makes "the suggestion of Mesoamerican chronology recuperates the Aztec and Maya cyclical nature of time, change, and growth."[70] Upon opening the accordion-like page layout that connect and unfold the story of the Conquest of the Americas is retold, reading each page as a visual codex left to right. It begins with Superman confronted with faux-traditional Mesoamerican imagery representing the eating of body parts and the drinking of blood by natives. Alongside these representations of cannibalism, an Aztec mythological figure also holds a plate with Mickey Mouse bound up as if prepared for mouse (human) sacrifice, a comically large salt shaker held above the exasperated mouse.

From this first page, the colonial narrative of civilizing the savages is presented with the heroic Superman and sympathetic Mickey Mouse confronted with a society in need of moral order. González notes in the introduction to the *Codex Espangliensis* that "[a]ction figures and cartoon icons stand in for the cultural imperialism perpetuated in commercial as well as political realms. Superman, Mickey Mouse and Wonder Woman join in a visual history of political oppression and exploitation that is both violent and seductive."[71] The satirical representation of the sacrificial practices of the Pre-Columbian indigenous indicts the stereotypical depiction of Mesoamerican culture that occupies the collective consciousness of mainstream audiences, reinforced by films such as *Apocolypto* (2006). Treating indigenous populations and culture as savage contributes to rhetoric of cultural deficiency, wherein ancient Latin@ culture is painted broadly as cannibalistic and ancient White culture is reduced to Greco-Roman history.

The presence of Mickey Mouse in this Pre-Columbian revisionist codex comes across as prophetic, given Disney's attempt in 2013 to copyright Dia de los Muertos imagery, to which poch@ pop artist Lalo Alcaraz responded. Still, with regard to contemporary popular media that fetishizes so-called "reality" and celebrity culture, there remain obvious similarities between Mesoamerican sacrifice and our historical moment's consumerist system of celebrity. *Schaden freud*, or the joy derived from seeing others in pain, could account in part for current genre-bending trends in news media and its precarious relationship with celebrity-driven paparazzi. The media industrial complex's process of icon-building of the famous and infamous parallels how the strongest of enemies were often the subjects of sacrifice. That the eventual downfall, and potential comeback in the case of celebrities, is a part of

DOI: 10.1057/9781137498076.0009

the formulaic narrative of the celebrity news cycle genre suggests the shared, communal role of mythos-creation. Even though the human sacrifice is the cliché simulacra for pre-Columbian culture, the lack of sympathy for celebrities portrayed as "melting down" does little more than isolate these figures to the point where their publicized failures, and sometimes deaths, may color how future generations judge this historical moment. Nericcio's meditation on Rita Hayworth's changing of name and lightening of hair and skin color demonstrates both a cultural sacrifice and death of ethnic identity in the name of mainstream success.[72] In *Codex Espangliensis*, Mickey Mouse stands in for icons of cultural domination, anticipating the erasure of culture through their mixing of pop and ethnic imagery. The fact that the pop icons are what makes a production like the *Codex Espangliensis* a consumable literacy object is a not so subtle indication for why poch@ pop artists cannot be afraid to engage in controversy—the colonial and neocolonial common sense of pop culture is too ideologically persuasive for mainstream audiences to distinguish their worldview from their ethical interpretation of issues like immigration, race, anti-immigrant legislation, and bans on anti-Ethnic Studies.

Over the next couple of pictographs, more traditional Aztec images dominate the visual landscape with Minnie Mouse, Superman, and Wonder Woman appearing in the margins, visually dominated by the native presence. Another panel displays the portrayal of Superman as hero to a Mexican youth, meanwhile in the adjacent codex, conquistadors overcome a chaotic population of indigenous within the mind of a silhouette without a face. A single image of Jesus wearing a crown of thorns with blood on his face alludes to the bloodshed of the European colonizers spreading the word of Christ through the spilling of pagan blood. These images seem to come down decisively on the question that John MacKenzie asked with regard to pop culture decades prior: "Were popular ideas merely a reflection of, or were they instrumental in, imperial policy?"[73] The presence of Superman, Mickey Mouse, and other pop culture icons step into the mythological role that religion once played, furthering colonial and neocolonial narratives. Because Gómez-Peña describes the *Codex Espangliensis* as a response to anti-Latin@ legislation in California, the depiction of colonial heroism echoes in the recent Arizona legislation that outlaws Mexican American history, while college credit continues to be awarded for Advanced Placement "United States" and European histories.

DOI: 10.1057/9781137498076.0009

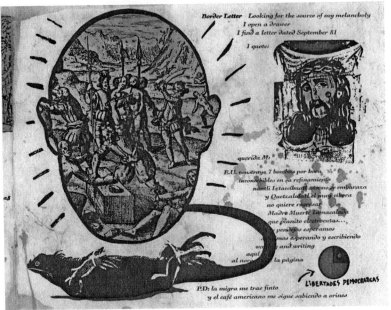

FIGURES 5.2A AND 5.2 B   *"Superman with boy; Jesus bleeding"*

DOI: 10.1057/9781137498076.0009

The (re)appropriation of Superman in not just the image with the young Mexican laborer among other laborers, but throughout the majority of the *Codex Espangliensis* symbolizes the message to assimilate in the U.S. In Superman's well-known origin story, he seeks asylum by seeking refuge—or *immigrating*—from the planet of Krypton to the U.S. where he adapts the customs and traits of his adoptive family, despite his alien status. Like many of the laborers in the image with the Mexican youth, Superman came to the U.S. at a young age because of turmoil at his place of origin. Like many of the undocumented students who would like to attend college, often referred to as Dreamers, Superman's parents made the decision to send Superman to Earth for a better life. Similarly, the quasi-red, white, and blue uniform that Superman dons exhibits his adoption of U.S. culture and ideology, communicating a visual message of U.S. allegiance and assimilation. That Superman is welcomed in the U.S. despite his "alien" status additionally underscores the discrimination against those who are racially marked by their ethnic difference in addition to their undocumented status.

In another panel, a self-assured stance demonstrates Superman's role as complicit with colonial power stands in stark contrast with the overwhelmed indigenous figures slaughtered by Mickey Mouse as an apparatus of the transnational hegemony. Mickey Mouse rides aboard a tank rolling through a circle of armed Aztec warriors, images of the Virgin Mary and Jesus hover overhead as visual spatial justification. The juxtaposition of pop whimsy with indigenous genocide highlights how the sacredness of Catholicism was invoked to commit godless acts against the poly-deism of Mesoamerican native populations. As a poch@ pop production, the *rascuache* (re)appropriation of popular sacred and secular imagery mirrors subversive rhetorical strategies of the pochteca. During the conquest of the Americas, the pochteca practiced subversion of colonial ideology when hegemonic practices came into direct opposition with indigenous culture.

Lockhart notes how pochteca used symbols significant to Nahua culture to (re)invent Christian objects introduced during the Conquest: "An anonymous annalist of Tenochtitlan in the 1560's tells of continuing corporate activity by the pochteca, noting that they decorated a Christian cult object with feathers and displayed a new saint's image in a procession."[74] Negotiating the oppressive European colonizers, the pochteca subverted colonial opposition by appropriating the figures, images, and symbols of the Christian world, yet reimagining and

DOI: 10.1057/9781137498076.0009

FIGURES 5.3A AND 5.3B   *"Superman crossed arms; Mickey Mouse tank"*

DOI: 10.1057/9781137498076.0009

appropriating them, in a quasi-*rascuache* methodology, into Nahua culture and belief system using artistic textiles.[75] To draw further on the overlapping roles of entertainment and ceremony, the subversive complicity that the pochteca perform, during and after the Conquest, parallel strategies performed by poch@ pop producers.

On a page underscored by the title of Gómez-Peña's "Radio Nuevo Orden," Catholic stigmata imagery of Christ's hand is positioned in relief to a cartoon hand that has an oil derrick spurting black and blue liquid from the same position as where nails would affix the hand on a cross. Once again overlaying religious imagery with pop culture iconography, Batman's logo rests beneath the oil-spurting hand that provides a foundation upon which the oil tower rests. In the visual rhetoric, the Batman oil company has come to replace the globalizing efforts of the Catholic campaign of the Spanish. The ideological messages embedded in capitalist imagery champion democracy and technological innovation rather than immortal afterlife, thereby distinguishing the religious colonial mission from the neocolonial agenda of capitalism.

Similar to the incorporation of Superman, the mythos of Batman provides context for the appropriation of this imagery. Batman's alter ego is billionaire Bruce Wayne, whose business holdings are on the whole consistently profitable, though the exact holdings are never exactly clear. Concerned with his metropolitan community, Batman fights crime locally in Gotham; however, as the owner of Wayne enterprises, Bruce Wayne is not held accountable for his role in globalization. One of the major fallouts of globalization continues to be the displacement of native populations, which is what took place in Latin American countries following the implementation of NAFTA and the re-writing of Mexico's constitution to evict the poor and indigenous from their lands. Baca notes the neoliberal criticism of policies that assuaged consumers of their role in exploitation:

> Written in English, Spanish, Spanglish, and Mexican-Spanish varieties, the poetic scripts critique Spanish colonization of the Americas, the North American Free Trade Agreement, and the consequences of globalization in the territories of immigration, language, and popular culture.[76]

Baca's point about globalization resonates particularly with this discussion of poch@ pop when considering the modern connotations of poch@ "*para nombrar a los 'otros mexicanos', a los que vivían más allá del Río Bravo* [for naming those 'other Mexicans', those that live all the way out near

DOI: 10.1057/9781137498076.0009

FIGURES 5.4A AND 5.4B   *"Batman stigmata; Aztec baseball glove"*

DOI: 10.1057/9781137498076.0009

the Rio Bravo]."⁷⁷ Along with the spread of pop culture across borders, the linguistic diversity in *Codex* has the rhetorical potential to challenge audiences who feel that "*los pochos como que no quieren ser mexicanos* [the pochos do not want to be Mexican]."⁷⁸ Because poch@s could live in northern states in Mexico, the poch@ identity has more to do with the spread of Anglo culture, a main export of globalization. No matter the medium of colonization, colonial messages of ethnic authenticity create a paradigm that poch@ pop artists de-mystify through their *mastery* of the colonial tongue and their re-configuring of pop symbols.

In a telling pictographic, a blood-covered Superman continues his embattled campaign of "civilizing barbarian" mobs, overseeing the lynching of natives and the suppression of Latin American revolutionaries. Deregulation in global business practices facilitates the institutionalization of exploiting indigenous and migrant workers as a part of common sense "inside-the-box" business ideology. A by-product of globalization is the deregulation of labor practices, all but erasing corporate responsibility for workers. The labor strikes and revolutionary action in Latin America share the same struggle of the subaltern against power, whether it is related to politics or capital. While Superman in this pictograph can be viewed as representing the spread of corporations, there is also the literal spread of pop culture through growing media networks that blur ideological boundaries through the inclusion of audiences south of the border. Juan Velasco notes that the warnings included in Gómez-Peña's work "point toward the dangers of commodification of indigenous and Latina/o identities into easily consumed pop culture products, and interrogate the redeeming potential of the poetics of hybridization in a world increasingly dominated by globalization."⁷⁹

Both in and outside the context of globalization, the issue of immigration remains a topos, or rhetorical commonplace, in borderlands rhetoric and rhetoric of the Americas because of the close relationship between the flow of capital and the demand for cheap labor. Considering the flow of popular culture, Américo Paredes describes its spread as the shifting of the border south: "[r]eading Mexican periodicals and listening to Mexican radio and television, one gets the impression that in a cultural sense the border has shifted south a bit, to the point somewhere below Mexico City."⁸⁰ Whereas the pochteca crossed over into foreign territories to trade and gather information, the work of poch@ pop artists formulates in part because of the transfer and negotiation of language through the globalizing spread of music, television, film, and comics.

DOI: 10.1057/9781137498076.0009

FIGURES 5.5A AND 5.5B   *"Mickey; Superman and mob"*

DOI: 10.1057/9781137498076.0009

In a telling juxtaposition of imagery, the Disney character Goofy stands atop a Mesoamerican skeleton statue in another panel. Above Goofy's head, thought bubbles include an exclamation point and a question mark, simultaneously fearing and experiencing confusion about the social epistemic and cultural memory upon which he treads. The image expresses the message that globalizing mainstream U.S. culture has very little understanding of the culture that it has covered over through projects of genocide and the destruction of codices bearing the histories in visual literacy. I hold with Emma Pérez's explanation that the validation of knowledge is a concern of historians recovering knowledge because previously marginalized knowledge and culture were made illegitimate by hegemonic power:

> Historical knowledge is the production of normative history through discursive practice…Oral tradition, codices, and archaeological remnants are only a few of the tools for studying pre-Colombian history in the Americas, and these methods are often considered illegitimate by traditional historians.[81]

Reading written history as a rhetorical production, the hegemonic agenda of establishing a dominant narrative becomes apparent, particularly at the cost of excluding other ways of knowing.

Furthermore, the juxtaposition and pairing of Mesoamerican and Disney symbols expose the argument that pairs mask resistant power in Pre-Columbian rhetorical productions.[82] However, the pairing of similar and disparate symbols has also provided a consistent method for identifying rhetoric in popular culture. In *Rhetoric of Popular Culture* Barry Brummett explains that "texts may put together signs that are not ordinarily found together. The match-up of those signs startles or jars us; it is from the potential conflict of signs that the unexpected pairing (and thus, pairing of unexpected meanings) gain rhetorical strength."[83] Reinforcing hegemonic expectations, Brummett reminds us that unexpected pairings can serve to omit racial and ethnic groups not represented in pop culture. As a result, audiences are indoctrinated to believe that people of color neither occupy visible positions in the material world, nor should viewers of color aim to fill positions of authority and prestige. The rhetorical power of pop culture is governed by ideological underpinnings that make it nearly impossible for producers who are unconscious of the gate-keeping enacted on non-dominant representations to succeed or overcome these exclusionary mechanisms.

DOI: 10.1057/9781137498076.0009

FIGURES 5.6A AND 5.6B   *"El Existentialist Mojado; Goofy"*

DOI: 10.1057/9781137498076.0009

Conclusion

The reasonably minor attention dedicated to the *Codex Espangliensis*[84] attests to the guarded walls of the ivory tower, where the neocolonial measures of a field's scope protect against the perceived "unworthiness" of subaltern subject matter. These standards of taste and aesthetic value reinforce the very same borders of bourgeois sensibility that make crossing over to mainstream audiences precarious for poch@ pop artists, even in the disguise of assimilation. The trope of poch@ has strong implications with assimilation given the growing number of Latin@s born in the U.S.; however, the cultural mestizaje of border art and rhetoric make the distinction between assimilated and resistant rhetorical productions blurred. When non-critical audiences read the work of Gómez-Peña, Lalo Alcaraz, George Lopez, Edward James Olmos, and Al Madrigal as espousing assimilation, these audiences fail to recognize the gaps and spaces in the border to crossover mainstream audiences and media that have been hacked open and widened through critical invention and (re)appropriation.

Modern re-imagining such as the *Codex Espangliensis* reveal important connections between contemporary pop culture and the rhetorical literacy practiced by the pre-Columbian indigenous. These connections not only provide porous sites of analysis between interdisciplinary borders, but they also provide poch@ artists and audiences with new ways of imagining the impact of assimilation on identity. Among the numerous connections between poch@ and pochteca, Richard Townsend's discussion of the disguises used by the pochteca hint at contemporary changes by mainstream Latin@ performers. In *The Aztecs*, Townsend explains that the disguised merchants were a subgroup of the pochteca called "the naualoztomeca, or 'disguised merchants,' trader-spies whose development as a special type of merchant at the service of the state . . . Naualoztomeca began as ordinary travelers who were obliged to disguise themselves as natives when entering enemy territories in search of rare goods."[85] Outside of the Mesoamerican rhetorical context, changes in appearance by "ethnic" performers like Rita Hayworth and Michael Jackson have been noted. Born Margarita Carmen Cansino, Rita Hayworth "successfully made the transition from ethnic minority to mainstream actress, a process that required her to lose her Latina identity, including changing her surname to Hayworth."[86] Poch@ subversive complicity is informed by the disguises of the pochteca who remind us that cultural identity runs deeper than hair style.

It is obvious and somewhat reductive to evaluate the radical changes made by pop culture figures to their physical appearance as some kind of authenticity indicator, as though there were such a thing. Both studies of the media and rhetorical studies remind us to ask, who is the audience? And, what appeals are made in the attempt to persuade this audience? In the case of mainstream crossover successes such as Hayworth, it has been argued that she attempted to mutate into the seductive hallucination of Latin@ identity, which white U.S. audiences constructed for "fiery" Latinas.[87] So I argue that the work of poch@ pop artists is that much more necessary, given the history and tradition of misrepresentation by Latin@s in mainstream media depictions.

Productions by poch@ pop artists help the effort of examining culturally relevant texts in mainstream scholarship where the concentric circles of poch@ pop consumers and scholars overlap, thereby decolonizing the narratives about Latin@s in the U.S. Incidentally, I agree with Juan Velasco summation of crediting Gómez-Peña's work such as the *Codex Espangliensis* for moving "the term 'border art' to the center, simultaneously exploring the complexities of the rich cultural and ethnic past of Latinas/os in the United States."[88] When terms like border art and poch@ become familiar for mainstream audiences, the rhetoric that they express and resist reaches broader audiences, for whom cultural deficiency narratives have often been normalized as part of historical fictions and myths of white superiority. Exposure to poch@ pop rhetorical productions challenges the next generation of Latin@s in the U.S. to disrupt, contest and further break from neocolonial narratives.

Just as I have examined the pop culture productions that I recognize as proto-poch@ and poch@, I believe that the attention to and normalization of resistant rhetoric to political messages and media representations of deficiency should, and will, continue. I bring these issues and topoi to the center of academic attention in much the same way that Greco-Roman culture has signified sites of history, philosophy, and rhetoric by Western academics, by pointing to the material cultural productions that have become imprinted in my memory and the collective memory of many Latin@s in the U.S. Also, the rhetorical imagery of the Americas operationalizes generative themes from the historical figures and tropes, thereby unlocking the potential for a re-imagined future of poch@ pop consumers.

DOI: 10.1057/9781137498076.0009

Notes

1   Gómez-Peña 1996, 24.
2   Anzaldúa 1987; Rodriguez 1983; Villarreal 1959.
3   Baca 2008.
4   Baca 2008, 29.
5   Baca 2008.
6   The American Civil Liberties Union (ACLU) reports copycat laws in the states mentioned with lawsuits filed in each state by the ACLU and others.
7   Nericcio 2007.
8   Wilson 1946, 345.
9   According to *Real Academia Español*,"pocho, cha. (Voz expr.). 1. adj. Descolorido, quebrado de color. 2. adj. Dicho especialmente de la fruta: Que está podrida o empieza a pudrirse. 3. adj. Dicho de una persona: Floja de carnes o que no disfruta de buena salud. 4. adj. Muy bueno, excelente. 5. adj. *Méx.* Dicho de un mexicano: Que adopta costumbres o modales de los estadounidenses. U. t. c. s." (http://buscon.rae.es/draeI/SrvltConsulta?TIPO_BUS=3&LEMA=pocho) July 5, 2011.
10   Wilson 1946, 345.
11   Nericcio 2007, 41.
12   Nericcio 2007, 78.
13   Villanueva 1997, 186.
14   Fanon 1967.
15   Anzaldúa 1987; Urrieta 2009.
16   Villarreal 1959, 64.
17   Villarreal 1959, 149–151.
18   Aldama 2005; Nericcio 2007; Villanueva 1993; Young 2004.
19   Nericcio 2007, 144.
20   Rodriguez 1982, 30.
21   Anzaldúa 1987, 77.
22   Anzaldúa 1987, 78.
23   Baca 2010, 144.
24   Villanueva 1993, 10.
25   Gómez-Peña, Chagoya and Rice 2000, i.
26   Wilson 1942.
27   Pérez 1999.
28   Mao 2003, 401.
29   Carrasco 1992, 176.
30   Leyva 2002, 10.
31   Paredes qtd. in Olguin 2005, 91.
32   *Pocho Handbook* 1980.

DOI: 10.1057/9781137498076.0009

33   Acosta 1945; Berdan 2005; German 1974; Kristan-Graham 1993; Townsend 2000.

34   Acosta 2007.

35   *Pocho Handbook* 1980, ii.

36   Rodriguez 1982, 26.

37   Baca 2008; Baca and Villanueva 2010.

38   *Pocho Handbook* 1980, 20.

39   *Pocho Handbook* 1980, 26.

40   Lockhart 1992, 192.

41   Townsend 2000, 195.

42   Wilson (1946) and Rodriguez (1982) define pocho as "discolored," and "bland" and "colorless" respectively.

43   According to *Real Academia Español,*"pocho, cha. (Voz expr.). 1. adj. Descolorido, quebrado de color. 2. adj. Dicho especialmente de la fruta: Que está podrida o empieza a pudrirse. 3. adj. Dicho de una persona: Floja de carnes o que no disfruta de buena salud. 4. adj. Muy bueno, excelente. 5. adj. *Méx.* Dicho de un mexicano: Que adopta costumbres o modales de los estadounidenses. U. t. c. s." (http://buscon.rae.es/draeI/SrvltConsulta?TIPO_BUS=3&LEMA=pocho) July 5, 2011.

44   Even though the geographic location I focus on is the United States, it is worth noting this early use of poch@ near the US-Mexico border and how "discolored" was generally used in relation to fruit, no doubt stemming from the pochotl tree.

45   While pocho with an "o" is used instead of pocha or poch@, this discussion is meant to address a phenomenon experienced by all genders.

46   Baca 2008, 64.

47   Gómez-Peña, Chagoya, and Rice 2000, vi.

48   Hill 1993.

49   Yosso 2002.

50   Kolodny 2008.

51   Baca 2008; Balsera 2005.

52   Léon-Portilla 2002.

53   Kristan-Graham 1993, 14.

54   Editor's brackets, Sahagún 1950, 21.

55   Acosta 1945; Berdan 2005; German 1974; Kristan-Graham 1993; Townsend 2000.

56   Sahagún 1950, 22.

57   Lockhart 1992, 100.

58   Lockhart 1992, 192.

59   Abbott 1987.

60   Villanueva 1997, 184.

61   American Indian rhetorical scholar, Malea Powell (2002), makes a similar accusation about the field, arguing it is "deliberately unseeing its participation in imperialism, both that of Great Britain and the United States" (p. 398).

62   Paredes 1993, 47.

63   Gómez-Peña, Chagoya and Rice 2000, ii.

64   Baca 2008, 64.

65   Baca 2008, 4.

66   Baca 2008, 11.

67   Baca 2008, 11.

68   Sahagún 1950, 24.

69   Berdan 2005, 36.

70   Baca 2008, 83.

71   Gómez-Peña, Chagoya and Rice 2000, iii.

72   Nericcio 2007.

73   MacKenzie 1986, 10.

74   Lockhart 1992, 192.

75   For a more in-depth discussion of subverted Christian symbols by Nahua, see Viviana Díaz Balsera's (2005) *The Pyramid under the Cross: Franciscan Discourses of Evangelization and the Nahua Christian Subject in Sixteenth-century Mexico.*

76   Baca 2008, 64.

77   Author's translation Maciel 2000, 84.

78   Valenzuela-Arce 2004, 130.

79   Velasco 2002, 208.

80   Paredes 1993, 47.

81   Pérez 1999, 7–8.

82   Baca 2008.

83   Brummett 2006, 123.

84   Austin and Montiel 2012; Baca 2008; Emerson 2008.

85   Townsend 2000, 196.

86   Tatum 2000, 53.

87   Nericcio 2007.

88   Velasco 2002, 208.

DOI: 10.1057/9781137498076.0009

6

Poch@s Strike Back: Ozomatli Members Respond to Pop Culture Commentary

Abstract: *Chapter 6 is a pop culture artists-speak-back interview with two of the founding members of the hip-hop cumbia fusion group Ozomatli, Raul Pacheco and Ulisses Bella. This chapter includes questions that address rhetorical aspects of composing, working within hegemonic systems, and socially-conscious decision-making. The poch@ artists respond to and discuss expectations of audiences and labels, as well as their role as cultural ambassadors for the U.S. government.*

Medina, Cruz. *Reclaiming Poch@ Pop: Examining the Rhetoric of Cultural Deficiency.* New York: Palgrave Macmillan, 2015. DOI: 10.1057/9781137498076.0010.

One of the difficulties as an academic—like any interpreter of visual, auditory, or written discourses—is the uncertainty of whether the message received, understood, and evaluated aligns with the ethos, logos, pathos, and ideology of what was intended by the text or speaker. Guillermo Gómez-Peña's *Dangerous Border Crossers: The Artist Talks Back* resurfaces at different points in this book, and I return to interviews with Gómez-Peña, Lalo Alcaraz, and Robert Rodriguez as primary sources because the perspective "from-the-artist's-mouth" can supplement and add further nuance to hermeneutic projects such as this one.

As a scholarly bridge between previous work and this book, I wrote an article for *alter/nativas journal of latin American cultural studies* on the L.A. fusion hip-hop, Latin-jazz, funk, and rock group Ozomatli.[1] This article served as a conduit between the ways in which I had conceptualized mestiz@ and borderlands rhetoric in terms of Latin@ student writing,[2] and how these decolonial frameworks played out in the neocolonial paradigm of pop culture. Fortuitously, from my article on Ozomatli, the opportunity arose to interview two of the band's founding members: Raul Pacheco and Ulises Bella.

Ozomatli formed in 1995 in Los Angeles, and is a seven-piece band that incorporates an eclectic mix of rock, rap, cumbia, Latin-jazz, and danceable beats that earned them both a Grammy for best Latin Rock and Latin Grammy for Best Alternative Album in 2005. Their songs code-switch between English and Spanish and exhibit the translingual make-up of the multicultural group that is representative of their L.A. roots. They have toured with Carlos Santana and Maná, contributed songs for the Los Angeles Dodgers and numerous children's movies, and released an album for kids. Notably, they served as cultural ambassadors, touring in India, Asia, Eastern Europe, and Latin America on behalf of the Bush administration.

Following Frederick Aldama's interview methodology in *Spilling the Beans in Chicanolandia*,[3] I returned to my previous research on the band, my own article, and further research into the themes that re-emerge in *Reclaiming Poch@ Pop*. This was not a straightforward interview about their history as performed in Juan Bruce-Novoa's *Chicano Authors: Inquiry by Interview*[4] because I sought to hold up a mirror to what I meditated on in this book with the thoughts of Pacheco and Bella. At the same time, I approached this chapter with the motivation of conducting the interview as an "artists speak back" chapter where producers who I would categorize as poch@ pop have the space to set the record straight or fill in the disjunction between *what they mean and how they are understood.*

DOI: 10.1057/9781137498076.0010

On the format of the interview, I conducted the interview simultaneously with both Pacheco and Bella. I tried to best capture not only the most accurate transcription of the interview, but also the overlapping dynamic that comes with discussion among collaborators with a nearly 20-year history. In the past, I have written about the use of Twitter by Latin@ students to communicate more effectively and create support networks,[5] so it is fitting that I mention Twitter during the interview as a source of statements made by different members of the band. The social media of Twitter connects producers and consumers in more direct, and public, mode of communication, which has the potential to illuminate the positive messages of poch@ pop artists.

I met with them prior to an Oakland performance in support of their seventh studio album *Place in the Sun* (2014), so I begin with their present endeavor as a contextual acknowledgement of the *kairotic* moment.

CM: "Brighter" is a song from the new album that seems to carry the same energy as some of the past songs, but you guys are great about acknowledging that undertone that touches on...

RP: Darkness.

CM: Or critical hope. How do you feel like you guys continue to balance that critical hope with the energy? Does the music come first?

RP: Even those of us who are militant at times about things, as a group it's never framed in that sense. You know, we're not Rage Against the Machine. And I think our energy when we're together is kind of light. We're...more about getting along—so even our differences, and things that are more critical or more pointed in terms of pointing things out—we have a tendency to do it that [light] way. 'Cause we're like a dance band.

CM: Has there ever been pressure from outside the band to follow one genre or trajectory? And have you had to push back explaining that there's a reason for the fusion?

RP: Sure, sure. But even when we try, we really can't do it. We tried to do it on this record [*A Place in the Sun*], and we just ended up doing whatever we wanted. It just wasn't feeling natural.

CM: This definitely is a spectrum on this album where "A Place in the Sun" captures the summertime feeling, but then I love "*Tus Ojos.*"

RP: That song ["*Tus Ojos*"] is about his [Ulisses Bella's] grandma.

CM: [To Ulisses] Could you elaborate on that?

UB: It started off as a jam that we would do live, and the thing is that this particular jam that we would do in the middle of a cumbia—we'd always hit the crowd hard, so I was like "we got to make that fucking thing a song. We got to make it a song, we got to make it a song..." ad nauseam, right.

CM: So it was another situation where the music came first?

DOI: 10.1057/9781137498076.0010

UB: The music came first, and then after that, my grandmother in *México*—I guess it was two or three years ago—she passed away. She was like 97. She could still speak her native language Otomí. And I just started writing lyrics and Raul [Pacheco] kind of helped out with it, and it all worked out.

CM: In my book about poch@ pop, I'm looking at people like Lalo Alcaraz. (To Ulisses) I know you're a Lalo Alcaraz fan because on Twitter, you said you were going to teach him some jujitsu because of the knuckleheads who were saying things to him.

UB: Lalo gets a lot of hate mail.

RP: (laughs) It's his job though. His job is a satirist.

CM: He stirs the pot a little bit.

UB: He stirs the pot big time and I like it.

CM: What I love about him is how he talks about his work as being a "political taco." I have the politics in there, but I have stuff on the outside that looks chipper with Disney pictures, even though he's calling Disney out for trying to trademark Dia de los Muertos.

UB: Right.

RP: Yeah, that was a trip.

CM: Raul, you said you had some links back to politics in Sacramento, and it seems you guys have been good in terms of maintaining connections with social issues. When you guys were Todos Somos Marcos, you guys said "If you need a house band for your political stances [we're your band]"—how have you been able to maintain that throughout your career?

RP: I was just think that as individuals, there's a make up of people, and there's enough of us who care about those things, who speak up about those things. You know yesterday, I was hanging out with some artists from here [Oakland], who were heavily involved with bringing to light issues of undocumented people, so it's just that all of have different kinds of friends, having all kinds of concerns, and it comes out in the songs. So I don't think it's forced or something. It comes naturally as what goes on for some of us. As a group, it's what's in there.

CM: One of the big political issues right now is immigration and it's that irony that you've mentioned before that you were the cultural ambassadors for the Bush administration, but then Barack Obama has been deporting people at a much higher rate. Did you get a lot of pushback for being cultural ambassadors?

RP: We got some.

UB: You know what's weird is that I was expecting a lot more, but a lot of people were actually really, really happy that something cool was actually being represented.

RP: It was just our Commie friends (laughs).

UB: Only the most hardcore, hardcore of the ultra-commies were like bummed out about it. But even then…It's funny that one of the last ones we did as a part of the whole ambassadorship thing was we played in Lithuania, and

DOI: 10.1057/9781137498076.0010

this gentleman showed up and we hung out with him afterward at the bar-drinking and whatever—and he was like, "Can I tell you something?" And I was like, "Go ahead, whatever." "You know when I first saw that the fucking embassy was going to bring Ozomatli here, I was like this is going to fucking suck. Like why would they do that? They're just going to be *this and that*. And then when I actually went to the show..." It's like I guess he just felt that it wasn't about the fucking embassy when he went to the show. It was just about us trying to connect and create our own story with the people there. It's like people are not dumb enough to think that just because a fucking band plays it's going to ease political tension or change foreign policy. And I mean if it did, maybe it would change it for the better because it was a declaration to the world that we have more in common than we have differences as far as we have in politics. One of the things that Raul always mentions is that some of the problems we face us here are some of the same problems that face other countries. Immigration is a global problem. It's not just us. Human rights is a global thing. I think that resonates.

RP: And I don't see it as a problem. I just see that inequity that forces people to get the hell out of one area and push into another. And to try and control that is really bizarre. I mean all of that is bizarre. But that's part of being human too. People have been getting together looking for food, moving places since the beginning of time, and it's the dynamic of that push. I think it's a bigger thing with countries—they're companies—countries are false kinds of units. They're more like companies, GDP [gross domestic product]. They're really about how much money you can generate and median wealth.

CM: I choose "(Who Discovered) America" [for the title of the article I wrote about the mestiz@ rhetoric of the band] because I think it's one of those great songs that's captures an anthemic sound, but there's critical undertones.

RP: We *do* do that a lot. That is a trick we do.

UB: We were touring with Kinky—they're this Mexican band from Monterey—and it was funny because they used to have this version [of "(Who Discovered) America?"] in which they used to go, "Ah, ah, America, *whatever*." (laughs)

RP: (laughs)

CM: Is language ever something like going straight forward in one genre, do you ever get that from one audience or another that wants straight English or just Spanish?

RP: Sometimes, yeah.

CM: Was that something that came up earlier, but now that you've had a long career...

RP: It's the same still.

UB: It's the same, but I think we are more flexible. We're just like *whatever*. [Because of] your fucking hang-ups about the language? I remember it used to be so much more militant about *not changing our shit*.

DOI: 10.1057/9781137498076.0010

RP: Like young artists are.

UB: Where now...

RP: You're like "yeah, whatever."

UB: Just play the fucking thing. Buy a record. Feed me (laughs).

RP: (laughs).

CM: (To Raul) In another interview, you talked about a commitment to social justice, and you mentioned being of service, making that decision to be of service and if people want that responsibility, they can be of service. Is that something you keep in mind when you're working with your label and they want you to do certain music?

RP: I think people think if you take stances, you can isolate an audience. I actually don't think that. I actually try to convince musicians that speaking up about certain things is profitable for your "brand." So I try to get them to think that speaking up about this stuff and doing these things—especially when it comes to helping people—most people think that's pretty positive. Doing something for kids—thinking that it's wasting your time? I think it's actually an investment, and if you are looking at it that way, there's actually a gain you get in people who might buy a CD, people who might come to your show. A whole group who see you differently because of that. It's like doing an interview. News organizations don't want to write the same old fucking stories. I think we've gotten a lot of play—*without trying*—from playing at teen homeless shelters. They think that is a cool story. I try to convince them [musicians] that if it's just business that it might help business too.

CM: I saw you most recently in Tucson, Arizona, because you guys were playing to support the Mexican American Studies program.

RP: At the Rialto.

CM: Yeah, I'm just supporting the point you're making because I got into you guys when I was young kid, being like "oh yeah, these guys kick ass," and then it happens that when I'm older and I know people who teach in the Mexican American Studies program, I was there for you guys in support of that too. To go back to being cultural ambassadors—[to Ulises] I know you said it's on your business card?

UB: I tell people, "I represent *you* homes."

CM: Did you guys ever get any flack from the state department or anybody who thought your music might have sounded subversive or did they just kind of dismiss it?

RP: I heard a few rumors, a few.

UB: Yeah. But first off, people in the foreign service are all kinds, are all types...

RP: A lot of them are hippies.

UB: A lot of them are hippies, a lot of them used to be in the Peace Corps. So we met some really, really cool, hip people...

RP: Who were in big positions.

DOI: 10.1057/9781137498076.0010

UB: So, sometimes you wonder, "wow, maybe this is some sort of weird, subversive thing that dudes are doing to get us." Obviously, when we first got the call, we were like, "are you fucking serious?" We were the first band to be against the war. We've been critical about the foreign policy for years. We're all pro-immigration. Motherfuckers are commies. But at the same time we might have encountered, I think, a little bit of ideological head-butting, but not much. One time, we were in Nepal, and this one woman was telling me—when we were going to have youth workshops—she was like, "try to convince the people that they shouldn't be striking all the fucking time. It shuts down." I was like, "You know I'm actually envious of them that they have that *power* to shut down the fucking country because we fucking sure can't get our shit together enough." Secondly, the destiny of the Nepalese people should be in their hands, not in foreign interests. So that kind of fucked that up between me and that lady for a little bit. There were little things here and there, but nothing crazy.

RP: Justin [percussionist and rap vocals] had an anti-Bush shirt.

UB: Justin had an anti-Bush shirt in Argentina, which is more of the anti-American vibe that we felt. But you know what? I want to say that like ninety-eight percent of the time it was all fucking good and all positive. Because of the type of people we are: we go to the place, we're not imposing anything, we want to learn, we want to absorb.

CM: What happened in terms of that? Did you guys decide to stop doing it [the cultural ambassadorship] yourselves?

UB: I think what it was, after a while, there was a little bit of internal conflict about it, and also it kind of got old.

RP: I think we got too defined by that. That was more the story. That was enough.

UB: We did our runs. We played some amazing fucking places, we got a ton of stamps on our passports, and connected with some unbelievable musicians and people. I mean stories for a lifetime. But after a certain point, okay, we got to go back to Ozo business.

CM: I'm curious how you guys got involved with more politics.

RP: People were there from the get-go. People were involved with it before, and the band was just an extension of people's individual personalities.

CM: How do you avoid burnout in terms of politics?

RP: I don't take all that shit too seriously. Most of the stuff you hear in the news is so broad—it's more for ratings. It's like the fight they pretend to have on TV (laughs).

CM: So do you end up getting more energy when you're able to go and do some of those events?

RP: Those are nice, they feel good, and it's not a chore. If we're organizing or doing something with kids, or for a certain issue, it's cool. People are usually really appreciative, and I think that just feels good. We're here, this is what

DOI: 10.1057/9781137498076.0010

we do. We sing and play songs. In those situations, I tend to feel like we're just giving people some relief and some energy. They're probably doing harder work in the day on a regular basis.

CM: Yeah, that makes me think of a video I saw you do for a social justice group.

RP: Everyone needs relief and fun. Real activists who work and commit their lives to that, they work pretty hard on that.

UB: It's pretty thankless too.

RP: You know they're not doing it for the money.

CM: With your work, you get to see people when they're in the mood to get their spirits lifted.

RP: I think a lot of times when we're doing that, we're a band, we're playing music, just getting people to kind of celebrate and let loose, feel energized.

CM: In the past you've mentioned writing in home studios and in jam sessions. What's a good way of describing your composing process?

RP: I think it happens all together and as an individual. I don't think there's a certain way we do it. It's just that everyone needs to like it.

UB: Whatever excites people the most in the end. You got seven dudes, so if you're the only one who's hyped by the idea, it's not going to fly.

CM: Still a democratic process.

UB: It's what excites the most people and then if everybody's like "oh yeah, that's the fucking jam." If everybody's on the same page about it, you know it's going to be good.

FIGURE 6.1   *Raul, Ulises, and Cruz*

DOI: 10.1057/9781137498076.0010

Notes

1   Medina 2014b.
2   Medina 2013a; Medina 2013b; Medina 2014a.
3   Aldama 2006.
4   Bruce-Novoa 1980.
5   Medina 2014b.

DOI: 10.1057/9781137498076.0010

Afterword

Medina, Cruz. *Reclaiming Poch@ Pop: Examining the
Rhetoric of Cultural Deficiency.* New York: Palgrave
Macmillan, 2015. DOI: 10.1057/9781137498076.0011.

▶

To return back to my personal experiences with pop culture, I think of Sherman Alexie's essay titled "I Hated Tonto (Still Do)" that appeared in the *Los Angeles Times*.¹ After reading this essay about Alexie hating the monosyllabic Tonto figure on screen that looked like him, I ruminated on my own pop culture personification, A.C. Slater from *Saved by the Bell* (1989–1993). Granted, Slater did not help the Anglo character Zack Morris hunt down Latin@ banditos; however, Slater's character still played the side-kick, and at times rival, jock who wasn't as smart (read: *tonto*) as Morris. The mocha-skinned actor, Mario Lopez, was always the first character to dance or issue a physical threat, all the while performing some kind of quasi-machismo by calling female characters "mama." Though less racist than Tonto, I resented Lopez's A.C. Slater even though the character learned in *Saved By the Bell: The College Years* (1993–1994) that his father had changed the family name from Sanchez to avoid discrimination when he joined the military. Too little, too late.

It's okay though. I always had Cheech. Since *Born in East L.A.* (1987) came out when I was seven, Cheech Marin has been there with me to laugh off those in Southern California who expected him to speak Spanish as he out-hustled the Tijuana border patrol. The low budget comedy addressed the not quite American, not quite Mexican bicultural experience that Anzaldúa was writing about at the same time. But Cheech let me and my family smile about those contradictions.

In his contributions to the *Huffington Post Latino*, Cheech Marin explains that self-identifying as a Chican@ contributed to his raised consciousness as an artist, growing from his early collaboration with Tommy Chong. Marin writes:

> It never bothered me until one day I thought to myself "Hey, wait a minute, I'm not Mexican." I've never even been to Mexico and I don't speak Spanish…No, I'm definitely not a "Mexican." Maybe I was "Mexican-ish"…Self-identification saved the day… A Chicano was someone who could do anything. A Chicano was someone who wasn't going to get ripped off. He was Uncle Rudy. He was industrious, inventive, and he wants another beer. So I got my Uncle Rudy another beer because, on that day, he showed me that I was a Chicano. Hispanic my ass, I've been a Chicano ever since.²

Like Marin, poch@ artists such as Lalo Alcaraz and Guillermo Gómez-Peña reflect the sensibility that cracks a biting joke with a wry smile with a critical issue in the set-up or the punch-line. Marin represents the generation of my parents who had few Chican@ and poch@ artists

DOI: 10.1057/9781137498076.0011

FIGURE A.1   *Medina and Marin*

speaking out on their behalf. But it was their generation who began the major excavations into the archaeology of recovering the knowledge, history, and culture that was covered over by the burning of codices, and which continues with the banning of books and programs benefiting Latin@s. My generation has the poch@ artists and producers I have discussed, in addition to those I have no doubt omitted for scope, and they provide strong voices of protest in response to rhetoric that attacks the humanity and spirit of Latin@s. The coming generations has poch@ role models who communicate resistant messages while seemingly fitting into mainstream systems of power—I envy this generation that does not have to settle for A.C. Slater because "he's better than nothing." I am hopeful that my children will not feel compelled to identify with Zack Morris even though he does not reflect their lived experiences.

Like Marin's uncle Rudy who asked for another beer, I hope this book reaffirms the strength of poch@ pop rhetoric as well as reminds poch@ audiences that the struggle against dehumanizing rhetoric is ongoing. Poch@ pop passes out political tacos at the sit-ins and demonstrations where poch@ tunes lift the heavy hearts and fists, pounding out the beat in time to the brush strokes of murals depicting the imminent demise

DOI: 10.1057/9781137498076.0011

of the global DC and Disney empires. Whether it was Dolores Huerta or Edward James Olmos—as it was in my pop culture imaginary—who uttered the now famous activist mantra, I say *sí poch@s pueden.*

Notes

1   Alexie 1998.
2   Marin 2012.

DOI: 10.1057/9781137498076.0011

Bibliography

Abbott, Don P. "The Ancient Word: Rhetoric in Aztec Culture." *Rhetorica.* 5.3 (1987): 251–264. Print.

Acosta, Curtis. "Developing Critical Consciousness: Resistance Literature in a Chicano Literature Class." *The English Journal.* 97.2 (2007): 36–42. Print.

——. Personal interview. May 2, 2012.

Acosta, Saignes M. *Los Pochteca: Ubicación De Los Mercaderes En La Estructura Social Tenochca.* México, D.F, 1945. Print.

Acuña, Rudolpho. "The Crabs." Mexi-can. org. Jun. 28, 2013. Web. Mar. 26, 2013.

Alambrista: (The Illegal). KCET Television, 1979. DVD.

Alcaraz, Lalo. "How Viva Obama Came About." *Aztlán.* 34.2 (2009): 205–208. Print.

——. *Laloalcaraz.com.* Web. Nov. 2, 2013.

——. *Migra Mouse: Political Cartoons on Immigration.* New York: RDV Books/Akashic Books, 2004. Print.

Alcaraz, Lalo ed. *Pocho.com.* Pochismo, Inc. Web. Nov. 1, 2013.

Aldama, Frederick L. "Review: Dangerous Border Crossers: the Artist Talks Back." *Modern Drama.* 45.1 (2002): 180. Print.

——. *Spilling the Beans in Chicanolandia: Conversations with Writers and Artists.* Austin: University of Texas Press, 2006. Print.

——. *Your Brain on Latino Comics: From Gus Arriola to Los Bros Hernandez.* Austin: University of Texas Press, 2009. Print.

Alexie, Sherman. "I Hated Tonto (Still Do)." *Los Angeles Times.* Jun. 28, 1998. Web. May 12, 2014.

Alt-Latino. National Public Radio, 2012–2014. Radio.

Amaya, Hector. "Citizenship, Diversity, Law and Ugly Betty." *Media, Culture and Society.* 32.5 (2010): 801–817. Print.

American Council on Education (ACE). "The Education Gap: Understanding African American and Hispanic Attainment Disparities in Higher Education." Nov. 28, 2012. Web. Dec. 1, 2012.

American Latino Television. American Latino Syndication, 2002–2014. Television.

Anzaldúa, Gloria. *Borderlands: The New Mestiza/La Frontera.* San Francisco: Spinsters/Aunt Lute, 1987. Print.

Aparicio, Frances R. "Jennifer As Selena: Rethinking Latinidad in Media and Popular Culture." *Latino Studies.* 1.1 (2003): 90–105. Print.

Arellano, Gustavo. "Ask a Mexican." *Orange County Weekly,* 2004–2014. Print.

Austin, K, and C.U. Montiel. "Codex Espangliensis: Neo-Baroque Art of Resistance." *Latin American Perspectives.* 39.3 (2012): 88–105. Print.

"Average Weather for Phoenix." *Weather.com.* The Weather Channel. n.d. Web. Oct. 19, 2013.

Avila-Saavedra, Guillermo. "Ethnic Otherness Versus Cultural Assimilation: U.S. Latino Comedians and the Politics of Identity." *Mass Communication and Society.* 14.3 (2011): 271–291. Print.

Baca, Damián. *Mestiz@ Scripts, Digital Migrations and the Territories of Writing.* New York: Palgrave Macmillan, 2008. Print.

Baca, Damián and Victor Villanueva. *Rhetorics of the Americas: 3114 BCE to 2012 CE.* New York: Palgrave Macmillan, 2010. Print.

Báez, Jillian M. "Towards a Latinidad Feminista: the Multiplicities of Latinidad and Feminism in Contemporary Cinema." *Popular Communication.* 5.2 (2007): 109–128. Print.

Balsera, Viviana D. *The Pyramid Under the Cross: Franciscan Discourses of Evangelization and the Nahua Christian Subject in Sixteenth-Century Mexico.* Tucson: University of Arizona Press, 2005. Print.

Barthes, Roland, and Annette Lavers. *Mythologies.* New York: Hill and Wang, 1972. Print.

Beltran, Mary. "The Hollywood Latina Body As Site of Social Struggle: Media Constructions of Stardom and Jennifer Lopez's 'Cross-Over Butt.'" *Quarterly Review of Film and Video.* 19.1 (2002): 71–86. Print.

DOI: 10.1057/9781137498076.0012

Berdan, Frances. *The Aztecs of Central Mexico: An Imperial Society.* Belmont, California: Thomson Wadsworth, 2005. Print.

Berlin, James. "Rhetoric and Ideology in the Writing Class." *College English.* 50.5 (1988): 477–494. Print.

Bhabha, Homi K. *The Location of Culture.* London: Routledge, 1994. Print.

Bourdieu, Pierre. *Outline of a Theory of Practice.* Cambridge, U.K: Cambridge University Press, 1977. Print.

Bourdieu, Pierre, and Jean-Claude Passeron. "Cultural Capital and Pedagogic Communication." *Reproduction in Education, Society and Culture.* London: Sage Publications, 1990. 71–106. Print.

Breidenbach, Carla. "Pocho Politics: Language, Identity, and Discourse in Lalo Alcaraz's La Cucaracha." *Linguistics and the Study of Comics.* Ed. Frank Bramlett. New York: Palgrave Macmillan, 2012: 210–238. Print.

Broyles-González, Yolanda. *El Teatro Campesino: Theater in the Chicano Movement.* Austin: University of Texas Press, 1994. Print.

Brummett, Barry. *Rhetoric in Popular Culture.* Thousand Oaks, Calif: Sage Publications, 2006. Print.

Burke, Kenneth. *A Grammar of Motives.* Berkeley, California: University of California Press, 1969. Print.

——. *A Rhetoric of Motives.* New York: George Braziller, Inc, 1950. Print.

——. "Terministic Screens." *Language as Symbolic Action: Essays on Life, Literature, and Method.* Berkeley, California: University of California Press, 1966: 44–62. Print.

Cabrera, Nolan L., Elisa L. Meza, Andrea J. Romero, and Roberto C. Rodriguez. "'If There Is No Struggle, There Is No Progress': Transformative Youth Activism and the School of Ethnic Studies." *Urban Review: Issues and Ideas in Public Education.* 45.1 (2013): 7–22. Print.

Cabrera, Nolan, Jeffrey F. Milem, and Ronald W. Marx. "An Empirical Analysis of the Effects of Mexican American Studies Participation on Student Achievement within Tucson Unified School District." University of Arizona College of Education. Jun. 20, 2012. Web. Oct. 10, 2013.

Calafell, Bernadette M., and Fernando Delgado. "Reading Latina/o Images: Interrogating Americanos." *Critical Studies in Media Communication.* 21.1 (2004): 1–24. Print.

DOI: 10.1057/9781137498076.0012

Calle 13. "Latinoamérica." *Entre Los Que Quieran*. Sony Music Latin, 2010. CD.

Calvo, Luz. " 'Lemme Stay, I Want to Watch': Ambivalence in Borderlands Cinema." *Latino/a Popular Culture*. Eds. Michelle Habell-Pallán and Mary Romero. New York: New York University Press, 2002: 73–80. Print.

Campbell, Kermit E. *Gettin' Our Groove on: Rhetoric, Language, and Literacy for the Hip Hop Generation*. Detroit, **Michigan**: Wayne State University Press, 2005. Print.

Carrasco, David, Moctezuma E. Matos, and Scott Sessions. *Moctezuma's Mexico: Visions of the Aztec World*. Niwot, Colorado: University Press of Colorado, 1992. Print.

Cintron, Ralph. *Angels' Town: Chero Ways, Gang Life, and Rhetorics of the Everyday*. Boston, **Massachusetts**: Beacon Press, 1997. Print.

Dangerous Minds. Perf. Michelle Pfeiffer. Hollywood Pictures, 1997. DVD.

De los Santos, René Agustín. "La Ola Latina: Recent Scholarship in Latina/o and Latin American Rhetorics." *Quarterly Journal of Speech*. 98.3 (2012): 320–336. Print.

Dead Poets Society. Perf. Robin Williams. Touchstone Home Video, 1989. DVD.

Deleuze, Gilles, and Felix Guattari. *A Thousand Plateaus: Capitalism and Schizophrenia*. Trans. by Brain Massumi. Minneapolis: The University of Minnesota Press, 1987. Print.

Díaz Balsera, Viviana. *The Pyramid Under the Cross: Franciscan Discourses of Evangelization and the Nahua Christian Subject in Sixteenth-Century Mexico*. Tucson: University of Arizona Press, 2005. Print.

Dickinson, Jennifer A. "Pocho Humor: Contemporary Chicano Humor and the Critique of American Culture." Diss. University of New Mexico, 2008. Print.

Douglas, N. "Purchasing Power at $223 Billion." *Hispanic*, December (1996): 48. Print.

Emerson, Melanie. "Hybrid Histories in Contemporary Artist Books: Codex Espangliensis and Doska Pocheta." *Museum Studies*. 34.2 (2008): 60–61. Print.

Enck-Wanzer, Darrel. "Trashing the System: Social Movement, Intersectional Rhetoric, and Collective Agency in the Young Lords Organization's Garbage Offensive." *Quarterly Journal of Speech*. 92.2 (2006): 174–201. Print.

DOI: 10.1057/9781137498076.0012

Ford, John, dir. *The Searchers*. Perf. John Wayne. Warner Bros, 1956. DVD.

Fregoso, Rosa L. *The Bronze Screen: Chicana and Chicano Film Culture*. Minneapolis: University of Minnesota Press, 1993. Print.

Freire, Paulo. *Pedagogy of the Oppressed*. New York: Continuum, 1993. Print.

Frida. Perf. Salma Hayek. Lions Gate Films, 2002. DVD.

Galeano, Eduardo, and Cedric Belfrage. *Open Veins of Latin America: Five Centuries of the Pillage of a Continent*. New York: Monthly Review Press, 1997. Print.

Garcia, Feliciano. "Robert Rodriguez, Alexa Vega and Danny Trejo Talk 'Machete Kills.'" *Cafecito*. NBC Latino. Oct. 2, 2013. Web. Oct. 31, 2013.

Garcia, Ramón. "Against Rasquache: Chicano Identity and the Politics of Popular Culture in Los Angeles." *Critica: A Journal of Critical Essays*. Spring (1998): 1–26. Print.

Gaspar de Alba, Alicia. *Chicano Art Inside/outside the Master's House: Cultural Politics and the Cara Exhibition*. Austin: University of Texas Press, 1998. Print.

Gates, Henry L. *The Signifying Monkey: A Theory of Afro-American Literary Criticism*. New York: Oxford University Press, 1988. Print.

German, Richard. *Pochteca and Other Professional Merchants of Late Post-Classic Central México*. MA thesis. UCLA, 1974. Print.

Ghanbari, Hazar N. "President Barack Obama and Jan Brewer." *Associated Press*. Jan. 25, 2012. Web. Oct. 2, 2013.

Gibson, Mel Dir. *Apocolypto*. Touchstone Pictures, 2006. DVD.

Girlfight. Independent Film Channel, 2000. DVD.

Giroux, Henry. "Book Burning in Arizona." *Truthout*. Feb. 8, 2012. Web. Jan. 12, 2014.

Go, Diego, Go!. Nick Records, 2007. CD.

Gómez-Peña, Guillermo. *Dangerous Border Crossers: The Artist Talks Back*. London: Routledge, 2000. Print.

——. "El Mexorcist 4: An Evening of Spoken Word Roulette." University of Chicago. Mandel Hall, Chicago, IL. Feb. 17, 2009. Performance Art.

——. *The New World Border: Prophecies, Poems, & Loqueras for the End of the Century*. San Francisco: City Lights, 1996. Print.

——. "The Virtual Barrio @The Other Frontier (or the Chicano Interneta)." *Clicking In: Hot Links to a Digital Culture*, Ed. Lynn Hershman Leeson. Seattle, WA: Bay Press, 1996: 173–185. Print.

DOI: 10.1057/9781137498076.0012

Gómez-Peña, Guillermo, Enrique Chagoya, and Felicia Rice. *Codex Espangliensis: From Columbus to the Border Patrol.* San Francisco: City Lights Books, 2000. Print.

Guzmán, Isabel M. "Mediating Frida: Negotiating Discourses of Latina/o Authenticity in Global Media Representations of Ethnic Identity." *Critical Studies in Media Communication.* 23.3 (2006): 232–251. Print.

Guzmán, Isabel, and Angharad Valdivia. "Brain, Brow, and Booty: Latina Iconicity in U.S. Popular Culture." *The Communication Review.* 7.2 (2004): 205–221. Print.

Guzman, Romeo. *Pocho in Greater Mexico.* Oct. 1, 2013. Web. Sept. 2, 2014.

Hernández, Daniel. *Down & Delirious in Mexico City: The Aztec Metropolis in the Twenty-First Century.* New York: Scribner, 2011. Print.

Hernández. Javier. *The Dead One/El Muerto.* Peninsula Films, 2007. DVD.

Hernández, Guillermo. *Chicano Satire: A Study in Literary Culture.* Austin: University of Texas Press, 1991. Print.

Herrera, Spencer R. "Pochoroman": The Birth of the Chicano/a Writer." Diss. The University of New Mexico, 2007. Print.

Hesford, Wendy S. *Framing Identities: Autobiography and the Politics of Pedagogy.* Minneapolis: University of Minnesota Press, 1999. Print.

Hill, Janet H. "Hasta La Vista, Baby: Anglo Spanish in the American Southwest." *Critique of Anthropology: a Journal for the Critical Reconstruction of Anthropology.* 13 (1993): 145–176. Print.

Holling, Michelle A. "Retrospective on Latin@ Rhetorical-Performance Scholarship: from 'Chicano Communication' to 'Latina/o Communication?'." *The Communication Review.* 11.4 (2008): 293–322. Print.

Holling, Michelle A, and Calafell B. Marie. "Identities on Stage and Staging Identities: Chicanobrujo Performances As Emancipatory Practices." *Text and Performance Quarterly.* 27.1 (2007): 58–83. Print.

Horne, Tom. "Arizona House Bill 2281." AZLeg.gov. May 11, 2010. Web. Jun. 15, 2011.

Hugo Lopez, Mark. "Three-Fourths of Hispanics Say Their Community Needs a Leader." Pew Research Center. Oct. 22, 2013. Web. Feb. 15, 2014.

Hurtado, Aida, and Carlos H. Arce. "Mexicans, Chicanos, Mexican Americans, or Pochos...que Somos? The Impact of Language and

DOI: 10.1057/9781137498076.0012

Nativity on Ethnic Labeling." *Aztlan: a Journal of Chicano Studies.* 17.1 (1986): 103–130. Print.

I Love Lucy. Perf. Desi Arnez and Lucille Ball. Columbia Broadcasting System, 1951–1957. TV.

Jameson, Fredric. "Reification and Utopia in Mass Culture." *Social Text* (1979): 130–148. Print.

Jencks, Christopher, and Meredith Phillips. *The Black-White Test Score Gap.* Washington, D.C: Brookings Institution Press, 1998. Print.

Keller, Gary D. *Hispanics and United States Film: An Overview and Handbook.* Tempe, Ariz: Bilingual Review/Press, 1994. Print.

Kelly, Andrew P, Mark Schneider, and Kevin Carey. *Rising to the Challenge: Hispanic College Graduation Rates As National Priority.* Washington, D.C.: American Enterprise Institute, Mar. 1, 2010. Web. Oct. 9, 2013.

Kennedy, George A. *Comparative Rhetoric: An Historical and Cross-Cultural Introduction.* New York: Oxford University Press, 1998. Print.

Kolodny, Annette. "Tropic Trappings in Mel Gibson's *Apocalypto* and Joseph Nicolar's *The Life and Traditions of the Red Man*." *American Indian Culture and Research Journal.* 32.1 (2008): 21–34. Print.

Kristan-Graham, Cynthia. "The Business of Narrative at Tula: an Analysis of the Vestibule Frieze, Trade, and Ritual." *Latin American Antiquity.* 4.1 (1993): 3–21. Print.

La Bamba. Dir. Luis Valdez. Perf. Lou Diamond Philips. Columbia Pictures Corporation, 1987. DVD.

Latination. Los Angeles: American Latino Syndication, 2004–2014. Television.

Latino USA. Futuro Media Group and National Public Radio, New York, 1992–2014. Radio.

Lee, Spike. *Malcolm X.* Perf. Denzel Washington. Warner Home Video, 1992. DVD.

León-Portilla, Miguel. *The Broken Spears: The Aztec Account of the Conquest of Mexico.* Boston: Beacon Press, 1992.

——. *Bernardino De Sahagún, First Anthropologist.* Norman: University of Oklahoma Press, 2002. Print.

Leyva, Yolanda Chávez. "The Re-visioning of History Es Una Gran Limpia: Teaching and Historical Trauma in Chicana/o History, Part II." *La Voz de Esperanza.* 15.7. Sept. 1, 2002. Web. Oct. 15, 2013.

Licona, Adela C. *Zines in Third Space: Radical Cooperation and Borderlands Rhetoric.* Albany, NY: State University of New York Press, 2012. Print.

DOI: 10.1057/9781137498076.0012

Lipka, Sara. "As Minority Students' Completion Rates Lag, a New Report Asks Why." *The Chronicle of Higher Education*. Nov. 28, 2012. Web. Dec. 1, 2012.

Lockhart, James. *The Nahuas After the Conquest: A Social and Cultural History of the Indians of Central Mexico, Sixteenth Through Eighteenth Centuries*. Stanford, California: Stanford University Press, 1992. Print.

Lunsford, Andrea A, and Lahoucine Ouzgane. *Crossing Borderlands: Composition and Postcolonial Studies*. Pittsburgh: University of Pittsburgh Press, 2004. Print.

Maciel, David. *El Bandolero, El Pocho Y La Raza: Imágenes Cinematográficas Del Chicano*. México, D.F: Conaculta, 2000. Print.

MacKenzie, John M. *Imperialism and Popular Culture*. Manchester, UK: Manchester University Press, 1986. Print.

Madrigal, Al. "Aliens vs. President: Immigration Reform." *The Daily Show with Jon Stewart*. May 18, 2011. Web. May 18, 2011.

——. "Tucson's Mexican-American Studies Ban." *The Daily Show with Jon Stewart*. Apr. 2, 2012. Web. Apr. 3, 2012.

Magill, R J. *Chic Ironic Bitterness*. Ann Arbor: University of Michigan Press, 2007. Print.

Mao, LuMing. "Reflective Encounters: Illustrating Comparative Rhetoric." *Style*. 37.4 (2003): 401–425. Print.

Marin, Cheech. "What is a Chicano?" *Huffington Post: Latino Voices*. May 3, 2012. Web. May 4, 2012.

Martinez, Aja. "'The American Way': Resisting the Empire of Force and Color-Blind Racism." *College English*. 71.6 (2009): 584–595. Print.

Mayer, Jane. "Covert Operations: The Billionaire Brothers Who Are Waging a War Against Obama." *The New Yorker*. Aug. 30, 2010. Web. Jun. 7, 2014.

Mayer, Vicki. "Living Telenovelas/Telenovelizing Life: Mexican American Girls' Identities and Transnational Telenovelas." *Journal of Communication*. 53.3 (2003): 479–495. Print.

Medina, Cruz N. "*Nuestros Refranes*: Culturally Relevant Writing in Tucson High Schools." *Reflections: A Journal of Public Rhetoric, Civic Writing, and Service Learning*. 12.3. (2013a): 52–79. Print.

——. "Poch[@]teca: Rhetorical Strategies of a Chican@ Academic Identity". Diss. University of Arizona, 2013b. Print.

——. "Tweeting Collaborative Identity: Race, ICTs and Performing Latinidad." *Communicating Race, Ethnicity, and Identity in Technical*

DOI: 10.1057/9781137498076.0012

Communication. Eds. Miriam Williamson and Octavio Pimentel. Amityville: Baywood Publishing, 2014a. 63–86. Print.

——. "'(Who Discovered) America': Ozomatli and the Mestiz@ Rhetoric of Hip Hop." *Alter/nativas* Spring, 2 (2014b): 1–24. Web. Mar. 26, 2014.

Medina, Cruz. Martinez, Aja, and Octavio Pimentel. "We are the .2%." College Composition and Communication Conference. Riviera Hotel, Las Vegas, NV. Mar. 14, 2013. Conference presentation.

Mesa-Bains, Amalia. "'Domesticana': the Sensibility of Chicana Rascuache." *Aztlán: a Journal of Chicano Studies.* 24.2 (1999): 155–167. Print.

"Naco, Pocho." *Mun2.* Telemundo. Jul. 1, 2012. Web. Jul. 22, 2012.

Nericcio, William A. *Tex[t]-Mex: Seductive Hallucinations of the "Mexican" in America.* Austin: University of Texas Press, 2007. Print.

Noriega, Chon A. *Visible Nations: Latin American Cinema and Video.* Minneapolis: University of Minnesota Press, 2000. Print.

Olguin, B.V. "Reassessing Pocho Poetics: Americo Paredes's Poetry and the (Trans)national Question." *Aztlán.* 30.1 (2005): 87–122. Print.

Olmos, Edward James, perf. *American Family.* Dir. Barbara Martinez Jitner. 20th Century Fox, 2002. DVD.

——. *American Me.* Dir. Edward James Olmos. Universal Studios, 1992. DVD.

——. *The Ballad of Gregorio Cortez.* Los Angeles: KCET Television, 1982. DVD.

——. *Battlestar Galactica.* Dir. Edward James Olmos. Universal Studios, 2004–2009. DVD.

——. *Blade Runner.* Dir. Ridley Scott. Warner Home Video, 1982. DVD.

——. *Miami Vice.* National Broadcasting Company, 1984–1990. DVD.

——. *My Family.* Dir. Gregory Nava. New Line Home Video, 1995. DVD.

——. *Selena.* Dir. Gregory Nava. Warner Home Video, 1997. DVD.

——. *Stand and Deliver.* Dir. Ramón Menéndez. Warner Home Video, 1988. DVD.

——. *Zoot Suit.* Dir. Luis Valdez. Universal Studios, 1981. DVD.

Olmos, Edward James prod. *Americanos: Latino Life in the United States.* Olmos Productions, 2000. DVD.

——. *El Americano: The Movie.* Olmos Productions, 2014. DVD.

——. *Filly Brown.* Olmos Productions, 2012. DVD.

One Eight Seven (187). Warner Home Video, 1997. DVD.

Outlawing Shakespeare: The Battle for the Tucson Mind. The Nonprofit Network, 2013. Web. Nov. 1, 2013.

DOI: 10.1057/9781137498076.0012

Precious Knowledge. Arizona: Dos Vatos Productions, 2011. DVD.

Papper, Robert A. *Local Television News Study of News Directors and the General Public.* Washington, DC: Radio and Television News Directors Foundation, 2003. Print.

Paredes, Américo, and Richard Bauman. *Folklore and Culture on the Texas-Mexican Border.* Austin, Tex: CMAS Books, Center for Mexican American Studies, University of Texas at Austin, 1993. Print.

Passel, Jeffrey S. and D'Vera Cohn. "U.S. Population Projections: 2005–2050." *Pew Research Hispanic Trends Project.* Feb. 11, 2008. Web. Mar. 26, 2014.

Pearce, Russell. "Arizona Senate Bill 1070." AZLeg.gov. May 11, 2010. Web. Jun. 15, 2011.

Pérez, Emma. *The Decolonial Imaginary: Writing Chicanas into History.* Bloomington, Ind: Indiana University Press, 1999. Print.

Pimentel, Octavio, and Paul Velazquez. "*Shrek 2*: an Appraisal of Mainstream Animation's Influence on Identity." *Journal of Latinos and Education.* 8.1 (2009): 5–21. Print.

Plato. *The Collected Dialogues of Plato.* E. Hamilton and H. Cairns (trs.), Princeton: Princeton University Press, 1978. Print.

"Pocho." *Royal Academy of Spanish/Real Academia de Español.* Oct. 22, 2011. Web. Nov. 2, 2012.

The Pocho Handbook. Los Angeles, Ca: Pocho Cultures Research & Development, 1980. Print.

Powell, Malea. "Rhetorics of Survivance: How American Indians Use Writing." *College Composition and Communication.* 53.3 (2002): 396–434. Print.

Raices De Sangre: Roots of Blood. Los Angeles, CA: Desert Mountain Media, 1977.

Ramírez-Berg, Charles. *Latino Images in Film: Stereotypes, Subversion, Resistance.* Austin, TX: University of Texas Press, 2002. Print.

Real Women Have Curves. Home Box Office Films, 2002. DVD.

Rodriguez, América. "Commercial Ethnicity: Language, Class and Race in the Marketing of the Hispanic Audience." *The Communication Review* 2.3 (1997): 283–309. Print.

——. *Making Latino News: Race, Language, Class.* Thousand Oaks, California: Sage Publications, 1999. Print.

Rodriguez, Richard. *Hunger of Memory: The Education of Richard Rodriguez: an Autobiography.* Boston, Mass: D.R. Godine, 1982. Print.

DOI: 10.1057/9781137498076.0012

Rodriguez, Robert, dir. *Machete Kills*. Universal Studios Home Entertainment, 2013. DVD.

——. *Desperado*. Columbia Pictures Corporation, 1995. DVD.

——. *El Mariachi*. Columbia Pictures Corporation, 1992. DVD.

——. *Once Upon a Time in Mexico*. Columbia Pictures Corporation, 2003. DVD.

Rodriguez, Robert and Ethan Maniquis, dir. *Machete*. Twentieth Century Fox Home Entertainment, 2010. DVD.

Rodriguez, Robert and Quentin Tarantino, dir. *Four Rooms*. Miramax, 1995. DVD.

——. *From Dusk Till Dawn*. Dimensions Films, 1996. DVD.

Rodriguez, Robert, Quentin Tarantino and Frank Miller dir. *Sin City*. Dimensions, 2005. DVD.

Rodriguez, Robert, Quentin Tarantino, Eli Roth, Edgar Wright, and Rob Zombie. *Grindhouse: Planet Terror and Death Proof*. Dimensions, 2007. DVD.

Romero, Anabell. "Entendiendo la 'Pocho' life en los USA." *Univision*. Mar. 27, 2013. Web. Mar. 26, 2014.

Rosales, Francisco A. *Chicano!: The History of the Mexican American Civil Rights Movement*. Houston, TX: Arte Público Press, 1997. Print.

Sahagún, Bernardino De, Arthur J.O. Anderson, and Charles E. Dibble. *General History of the Things of New Spain: Florentine Codex*. Santa Fe, N.M: School of American Research, 1950. Print.

Samuelson, Ruth. "No HABLA Español." *Columbia Review of Journalism*. Sept. 13, 2012. Web. Oct. 9, 2013.

Sandoval, Chela. *Methodology of the Oppressed*. Minneapolis, MN: University of Minnesota Press, 2000. Print.

Saved by the Bell. Perf. Mario Lopez. NBC Productions, 1989. Television.

Saved by the Bell: The College Years. Perf. Mario Lopez. NBC Productions, 1993. Television.

Schwartz, David. "Judge Orders Monitor Appointed to Oversee Controversial Arizona Sheriff." *Reuters*. Thomson Reuters. Oct. 2, 2013. Web. Oct. 9, 2013.

Seguín. KCET Television, 1981. DVD.

Serna, Elias. "Tucson and Los Angeles: Parallel Universes, 'Scattering Jade', and De-colonial Rhetorics." Rhetoric Society of America Conference. Marriot Rivercenter Hotel, San Antonio, TX. May 23, 2014. Conference presentation.

DOI: 10.1057/9781137498076.0012

Shakespeare, William. *The Tempest*. Cambridge: Cambridge University Press, 2013.

Shrek 2. Perf. Michael Meyers. Dreamworks, 2004. DVD.

Soto, Sandra K. *Reading Chican@ Like a Queer: The De-Mastery of Desire*. Austin: University of Texas Press, 2010. Print.

Spener, David. "Movidas Rascuaches: Strategies of Migrant Resistance at the Mexico-US Border." *Aztlán: A Journal of Chicano Studies*. 35.2 (2010): 9–36. Print.

Sprager, Della. *The Pochteca in Aztec Society: Trade Elite in Pre-Columbian Times*. Austin, Tex: s.n., 1978. Print.

Steele, Claude. *Whistling Vivaldi: And Other Clues to How Stereotypes Affect Us*. New York: W.W. Norton & Company, 2010. Print.

Subervi, Federico, Joseph Torres, and Daniela Montalvo. *The Portrayal of Latinos & Latino Issues on Network Television News, 2003: Quantitative & Qualitative Analysis of the Coverage*. Austin, Tex: National Association of Hispanic Journalists, 2005. Web. Mar. 1, 2014.

Tatum, Charles M. *Chicano Popular Culture: Que Hable El Pueblo*. Tucson: University of Arizona Press, 2001. Print.

Thackara, Tess. "Interview with Guillermo Gómez-Peña." *Art Practical*. Apr. 13, 2011. Web. Oct. 9, 2013.

That 70s Show. Perf. Wilmer Valderrama. 20th Century Fox, 2006. DVD.

The Latino List: Volume 1 and 2. New York: Home Box Office, 2011–2012. Television.

The Substitute. Dinamo Entertainment, 1996. DVD.

Torres, Edén E. *Chicana Without Apology: Chicana Sin Vergüenza: the New Chicana Cultural Studies*. New York: Routledge, 2003. Print.

Torres, Lourdes. "In the Contact Zone: Code-Switching Strategies by Latino/a Writers." *Melus: Society for the Study of the Multi-Ethnic Literature of the United States*. 32.1 (2007): 75–96. Print.

Touch of Evil. Orson Welles dir. Universal Studios, 1958. DVD.

Townsend, Richard F. *The Aztecs*. London: Thames & Hudson, 2000. Print.

Two Americans. Dan DeVito and Valeria Fernández dir and prod. 2011. DVD.

Ugly Betty. Burbank, CA: Walt Disney Studios Home Entertainment, 2006–2010. DVD.

Valdez, Luis. "*Tu Eres Mi Otro Yo*." *Zoot Suit and Other Plays*. Houston, TX: Arte Publico Press, 1992: 10. Print.

DOI: 10.1057/9781137498076.0012

Valdivia, Angharad N. *Latina/os and the Media*. Cambridge, England: Polity Press, 2010. Print.

Valenzuela, Angela. *Subtractive Schooling: U.S.-Mexican Youth and the Politics of Caring*. Albany: State University of New York Press, 1999. Print.

Valenzuela-Arce, Jose Manuel. "Fronteras Y Representaciones Sociales: La Figura Del Pocho Como Estereotipo Del Chicano." *Aztlán*. 29 (2004): 125–134. Print.

Vasconcelos, José, and Didier T. Jaén. *The Cosmic Race: A Bilingual Edition*. Baltimore, Md: John Hopkins University Press, 1997. Print.

Velasco, Juan. "Performing Multiple Identities: Guillermo Gómez-Peña and his *Dangerous Border Crossings*." *Latino/a Popular Culture*. Eds. Michelle Habell-Pallán and Mary Romero. New York: New York University Press, 2002: 208–224. Print.

Villanueva, Victor. *Bootstraps: From an American Academic of Color*. Urbana, Ill: National Council of Teachers of English, 1993. Print.

——. "Blind: Talking About the New Racism." *The Writing Center Journal*. 26 (2006): 3–19. Print.

——. "Maybe a Colony: and Still Another Critique of the Comp Community." *JAC: A Journal of Composition Theory*. 17.2 (1997): 183–190. Print.

——. " 'Memoria' Is a Friend of Ours: On the Discourse of Color." *College English*. 67.1 (2004): 9–19. Print.

Villarreal, José A. *Pocho*. Garden City, N.Y: Doubleday, 1959. Print.

Washington Heights. New York: Music Television, 2013. Television.

Wilson, William E. "A Note on 'Pochismo'." *Modern Language Journal*. 30.6 (1946): 345–346. Print.

Wegner, Kyle D. "Children of Aztlán: Mexican American Popular Culture and the Post-Chicano Aesthetic." Diss. State University of New York at Buffalo, 2006. Print.

Wood, Graeme. "Univision's English-Language News Network, Fusion, Targets Millennials." *Businessweek.com*. Bloomberg Businessweek Companies & Industries. Sept. 5, 2013. Web. Oct. 9, 2013.

Ybarra-Frausto, Tomás. "Rasquachismo: A Chicano Sensibility." *Chicano Art: Resistance and Affirmation, 1965–1985*. Eds. Richard Griswold del Castillo, Teresa McKenna, and Yvonne Yarbro-Bejarano. Los Angeles: Wight Art Gallery, University of California, Los Angeles, 1991. 155–179. Print.

Yo Soy Betty, La Fea. Colombia: RCN, 1999–2001. DVD.

DOI: 10.1057/9781137498076.0012

Yosso, Tara J. "Critical Race Media Literacy: Challenging Deficit Discourse about Chicanas/os." *Journal of Popular Film & Television.* 30:1 (2002): 52–62. Print.

Young, Morris. *Minor Re/visions: Asian American Literacy Narratives as a Rhetoric of Citizenship.* Carbondale: Southern Illinois University Press, 2004. Print.

DOI: 10.1057/9781137498076.0012

Index

DOI: 10.1057/9781137498076.0013

DOI: 10.1057/9781137498076.0013

DOI: 10.1057/9781137498076.0013